Without Stigma

Without Stigma

About the Stigma of
the Mental Illness

Darko Pozder

To order additional copies of this book, contact:
Xlibris
1-800-455-039
www.Xlibris.com.au
Orders@Xlibris.com.au
768820

CONTENTS

Chapter 1   History Of Mental Illness... 1

History of Mental Illness 2
Development of Mental Health Facilities.................................... 4
Hippocrates's Views of Mental Illness 5
Mental Illness in the Nineteenth Century.................................. 6
Signs of Mental Illness... 9
Neurotransmitters and Mental Illness..................................... 14
Types of Mental Illnesses 15
Management of Obsessive-Compulsive Disorder..................... 31
The Causes of Schizophrenia.. 33

Chapter 2   Stigma And Mental Illness..41

The Causes of Stigma towards Mental Illness 44
The Impact of Stigma Towards People Affected by Mental Illness...... 46
Impact of Stigma in the Workplace 48
Models of Mental Illness Stigma 50
The Types of Stigma 51
Ways of Reducing Public Stigma.. 54
Mental Illness and the Media... 61
How Social Media Can Positively Represent Mental Illness................. 72
How the Mass Media Can Positively Represent Mental Illness 74

Chapter 3   Stigma And Mental Illness - Part II 80

Rejection as a Result of Stigma towards People with Mental Illness ... 80
Stigma and Social Affiliation.. 84
Stigma and Loss of Identity.. 87
Cultures in Relation to Stigma Associated with Mental Illness........... 89
The Impact of Cognitive Closure on Mental Illness.......................... 101
Self-Medication due to Stigma Associated with Mental Illness 107

**Chapter 4   Early Intervention And Stigma In Relation
To Mental Illness** **116**

Reasons Stigma Hinders Early Intervention 117
Ways of Encouraging Early Intervention for Those Affected
by Mental Illness 119
Benefits of Early Intervention 122
Immigrant Families and Mental Illness 125
Breaking the Stigma of Mental Illness among the Immigrants 132
Media and Early Intervention of Mental Illness 138
Ways in Which the Wrong Misrepresentation by the Media of
Mental Illness Hinders Early Treatment 144

Chapter 5   Steps In Reducing The Stigma On Mental Illness............147

Educating Others.. 147
Attitude and Behaviour 153
Positive Counselling and Therapy 159
Training of Skills 163
Exploring Facts as a Step in Reducing Stigma on Mental Illness 165
Creating Coping Skills as a Step in Reducing Stigma on
Mental Illness... 168
Conceptual Models in Reducing Stigma on Mental Illness 175
The Basic Needs Model.. 179

Chapter 6   Psychoeducation **182**

The History of Psychoeducation 184
Ecological System Theory 184
Cognitive Behavioural Theory in Psychoeducation........................... 185
Group Practice Models in Psychoeducation 188
Narrative Approach Theory in Psychoeducation 189
The Stress and Coping Model in Psychoeducation 190
Psychoeducation Approaches 192
Common Topics in Psychoeducation 193
Objectives/Goals of Psychoeducation 194
The Importance/Benefits of Psychoeducation.................................... 194
The Categories of Psychoeducation 196
The Models of Psychoeducation... 208

Conclusion.. **209**

To my brother Marko, the hero of my life.

PREFACE

Without Stigma: About the Stigma of the Mental Illness first edition is a book that has tried to discuss mental illness briefly. The idea behind the book is to educate the society on various myths which are associated with mental illness.

Media has been viewed as a significant tool in educating the public on this disease. There are a lot of stigmas that are linked to mental illnesses, which mostly is a result of different cultural beliefs and views; to reduce the stigma, the public needs to receive accurate information regarding mental illness. The book also addresses the adverse impact that stigma has on those affected by mental illness and their families.

Chapter 1 discusses the history of mental illness; this chapter also looks into how the mental health facilities evolved and their development over the years. Chapters 2 and 3 look at the stigma that comes with mental illness, the types of stigma, and the ways of reducing the stigma. In chapter 4, the delay in early intervention for those affected by mental illness is discussed in detail. In chapter 5, various steps or strategies which can help in the stigma reduction are discussed in particular, and chapter 6 looks at the impact of psychoeducation on mental illness.

ACKNOWLEDGEMENTS

Thanks to all my colleagues and clients of Schizophrenia Fellowship of New South Wales.

Chapter 1

History Of Mental Illness

Introduction

Mental illness refers to mental disorders which are diagnosable and involve notable changes in a person's emotions, behaviour, and thinking. Mental illnesses can also be referred to as psychiatric disorders. These illnesses affect people of all ages, gender, social and economic status, race, religion, and background without discrimination. Mental illness can either be mild, such that the person is able to continue with their day-to-day life with minimal limitations, or severe, where the affected person has to be taken to the hospital for treatment.

Through the centuries, there have been radical changes in people's perception towards people affected by mental illness. Most of the changes can be attributed to the changing societal mentality and information about some of the conditions. Interestingly, these changes have redeemed the field of psychiatrists from a negative light to a brighter and more positive light.

The purpose of this book is to examine mental illnesses, the stigma that has been associated with them over the years, the treatment procedures which are available for mental treatment, and the ways to reduce the stigma related with these illnesses.

History of Mental Illness

Indications of the existence of mental illness can be found throughout history. However, the evolution of the illnesses has not been progressive or linear but rather rotative. Whether a behaviour is considered abnormal or normal mostly depends on the context set by a given environment making it dynamic and pegged on culture and time. In the past, those who exhibited behaviours that deviated from the expectations and norms were considered abnormal. Their conduct was mainly attributed to evil spirits in terms that alluded to mental illness. Culture and time defined the pattern of behaviour and the acceptable and unacceptable approaches.

Based on this traditional approach, the society developed a less cultural relativist view of abnormalities. Interestingly, they avoided the concepts that would evaluate the motive behind such behaviours and would pose any threat to the people around them. The cultural classification of abnormalities failed to consider the dynamics behind the patterns. Their major focus was on the nature of defect given by their norms and practices. If the person exhibited new traits which were unheard of, this qualified them to have an abnormality tag or brand.

Across the centuries, there have been three main theories on the causes of mental illnesses: psychogenic, somatogenic, and supernatural. Supernatural theories accredited mental illnesses to possessions by demonic or evil spirits, sins, displeasures of the gods, curses, eclipses, gravitation, and planetary events. Somatogenic theories attributed mental illnesses to the interruption of the physical functions caused by the illness, brain imbalance or damage, or genetic inheritance. Psychogenic theories centred their arguments on stressful or traumatic experiences, distorted perceptions, or maladaptive learned cognitions and associations.

Etiological theories of mental illness focus on the treatment and care accorded to those affected by mental illness. While time has changed and perceptions transformed, the methods of treatment procedures have largely remained the same. Different mental illnesses attract various methods and treatment approaches. Traditionally, the methods included exorcism and bloodletting to cleanse victims form the chaining spells. Evidently, there existed limited knowledge about these conditions and their causes. Most of the treatment procedures were faith-based deprived of any scientific input.

Traditionally, mental illnesses were thought to arise from either magic or were a result of divine punishment. Most people considered the disorders to be caused by supernatural powers to either punish or make a specified communication to an individual. The perfect instruments that underplay in most of the cases ranged from sorcery, evil eyes, or demonic possession; however, demonic possession was considered as the leading cause of these conditions. The common treatment procedure involved the use of sacrifices and enchantment spells.

Egyptian and Mesopotamia from 1900 BC labelled women who had mental conditions as being cursed by the gods. They believed the illness resulted from having a wandering uterus. According to Egyptian culture, they believed the uterus detached itself from its original position and got attached to vital organs, such as the chest cavity, causing these organs to malfunction (Alexander, 1996). To cure this, the Egyptians, and much later the Greeks, started using somatogenic treatment by the use of substances having a strong smell to enable the uterus to go back to its proper position.

In the mental hospitals, patients were treated through bloodletting, purging, or dousing them in either very hot or cold water. The purpose was to shock the patient's mind into normalcy. To bring back normalcy to the patient, threats, blisters, and restraints were used (Alexander, 1996). In Ancient Egypt, the treatment of mental illness was through activities which were recreational, which included dances and concerts, with a purpose of alleviating the symptoms of the ill person. The Egyptians also treated mental illness through the use of surgery.

In Mesopotamia, those who were affected by mental illness were treated using rituals which were religious since the illnesses were believed to have been caused by demonic powers. The Greek physicians did not agree to explanations that were supernatural regarding mental illness. The ancient Persians attributed mental illness to demonic possessions, but they paid closer attention to personal hygiene. In all their treatment procedures, they ensured that the victim remained in good condition free from dangerous infections. The Hebrews, on the other hand, held the belief that all kinds of illnesses, including mental illnesses, were a result of God's punishment for sin. They also believed demonic powers caused sicknesses.

Development of Mental Health Facilities

In the sixteenth century, hospitals and asylums were started for those individuals who were affected by mental illness. The first institution was opened in Europe. The purpose of these facilities was to provide homes and lock up those affected by mental illness, the homeless, the criminals, and those who were unemployed. The family of these patients brought them into the asylum to ease the burden of shame that the family had by being associated with the sick individual. The treatment of those affected by mental illness in these institutions was for physical ailments, such as bleeding and purging. Most of the staff in the asylum were neither trained nor qualified, which led them to treat those affected by mental illness who had no reasoning capacity as animals. The people affected by mental illness were regarded as being incapable of controlling their behaviour and were subjected to living in adverse conditions as they were not expected to protest. An example of this kind of facility is La Bicetre Hospital in Paris, where patients were kept in the dark cells with chains, allowing them only minimal movement that could enable them to feed. The patients were required to sleep while standing; the food quality was also poor. Also, the patients were not allowed any visitors except those people who gave them food; cleaning the rooms was rare. As a result, the patients had to sit where their waste was (Butcher, 2007). In an asylum in London referred to as Bedlam, people affected by mental illness were exhibited for a small amount of money from the public, while the others went to the streets to beg.

In the eighteenth century, protests arose from the miserable conditions in which the people suffering from mental illness were living. Between 1759 and 1820, Vincenzo Chiarugi, a physician from Italy, helped the public to humanely view the patients by removing their chains in St. Boniface Hospital in Italy. Vincenzo also promoted occupational training and good hygiene among the patients. In England, there were religious groups who brought about reforms, among them being William Tuke in 1732–1822. In America, the mental illness somatogenic theory led to various treatments for those affected by mental illness, which included tranquilliser chairs and gyrators. In the years which followed, there was the introduction of more procedures, namely the compassionate care and psychogenic treatment. In America, between 1840 and 1880, there was the establishment of mental hospitals.

Furthermore, in Paris, in 1792, Philippe Pinel introduced changes in the asylum where he started with La Bicetre Hospital in Paris. The patients were taken care of with kindness, the rooms they were staying in started being cleaned, and they were given a chance to get out of their rooms and do exercises. William Tuke founded York Retreat in 1796, where there was an emphasis on treating everyone, including those who were mentally ill, with kindness and compassion. The houses in the retreat were pleasant, and the patients could live there comfortably. The humanitarian movement spread across America in the 1800s; the treatment's focus was on the social, occupational, and individual needs of the patient. The emphasis was mainly on the development of the patient's spirituality and morals.

Though treatment about moral management was effective, it later failed because of several factors. One of the factors was the ethnic differences between the staff and patients due to immigration. Also, those who started moral management treatment did not train others. Eventually, a gap occurred by having untrained staff in the mental hospitals. With time, there were biomedical advances which led to the end of the moral management in treating those who were affected by mental illness. The next movement in the treatment of those with mental illness was on mental hygiene, where the treatment's focus was on the patient's physical health, but it disregarded the psychological issues which the patient had.

Hippocrates's Views of Mental Illness

During the fifth and third centuries, there was a new dimension of mental illness which came about by the Greeks. Hippocrates, a physician and a Greek philosopher, discovered that mental illnesses had everything to do with malfunctions in the body and that they were caused by a lack of the essential fluids of the body. Hippocrates, in his study of mental illness in 460–370 BC, dismissed the superstitious concepts by introducing practical explanations. He studied brain pathology and made different suggestions pointing to the imbalances of the body as the cause of mental illness. According to his analysis, the imbalances were in four essential fluids—black bile, blood, yellow bile, and phlegm—referred to as humours, which brought about the unique personality patterns in a person (Butcher, 2007).

According to Hippocrates, an individual who was too emotional had too much blood, and the suitable treatment was bloodletting. He went further to classify mental illness into four groups, namely, mania, fever of the brain, melancholia, and epilepsy. Similar to other philosophers and physicians of his time, Hippocrates believed that there was no shame associated with mental illness. During this period, those affected by mental illness received care from the members of their families, but the state did not contribute in their care.

Despite the fact that the treatments proposed by Hippocrates were becoming popular, some cultures still resisted the treatments and continued in their belief in supernatural causes for mental illnesses. These cultures resorted to traditional healing, such as the use of charms and spells. In the Middle Ages, the patients were given laxatives to restore their body's balance, which was a result of a humour (MacDonald, 1981). There was a particular diet given to those affected by mental illness, which included milk, salad, greens, and barley water (Porter, 1982).

Mental Illness in the Nineteenth Century

In 1856–1926, a psychiatrist named Kraepelin classified various mental illnesses. He differentiated schizophrenia (what he called dementia precox) from other types of psychosis. He also differentiated between paranoia and hallucination. In the late 1800s to early 1900s, Sigmund Freud helped develop psychoanalysis, where he stated that the mind of a person was divided into three parts, mainly the ego, the superego, and the id. He went further to say that the functions of the id were for basic desires of aggression and sex. The superego's function, which was conscious and unconscious, was to help a person deny the impulses of the id and live an upright life. The ego's function, on the other hand, was to mediate between a person's id and superego.

According to the psychoanalytic theory by Freud, anxiety was a result of the three parts of the human mind battling against one another; this brought the mental disorder. He further stated that if a person was able to come to terms with what their unconscious mind contained, they would get healing for the mental illness (Myers, 2007). With time, the psychoanalysis failed, and Freud turned to free association where the patients were asked to relax and share any thought that came to their minds, however insignificant or shameful they seemed. He held the belief that the patients' thoughts would make a way to trail the patients' unconscious thoughts to bring back the thoughts and feelings that were repressed.

Freud also analysed dreams in treating those who were affected by mental illness. The patients were required to put a record of the dreams they had. A psychoanalyst would then study the dreams and look for content which was in the unconscious part of the mind as it was considered that the conscious mind was censoring the dreams and converting them to symbols.

During the same period, mental illness was being treated through psychopharmacology, psychosurgery, and electroconvulsive therapy. The treatments were based on the fact that mental illness was caused by the body having a biochemical imbalance. Thus, somatic therapy was to treat the mind by correcting the chemical imbalance in the patient. In 1938, shock therapy was introduced in treating schizophrenia, and it was successful; the treatment spread widely and was used mostly in Europe and America. Some mental or psychiatric hospitals abused shock therapy which used electricity in intimidating, punishing, and controlling the patients. The treatment has undergone major reforms and is still being employed in the modern times in treating patients suffering from severe depression. The treatment is used when the patient does not seem to respond to any other treatment.

Before the electroconvulsive therapy begins, the patient is given a relaxant for the muscle and is put under general anaesthesia to avoid danger which could include fracturing their bones. This kind of therapy is administered to the patient thrice in one week until twelve sessions are over. The adverse effects of this therapy to the patient are amnesia and disorientation for some hours before and after the session. At times, the electroconvulsive therapy was ineffective, and the patients resorted to psychosurgery, which was developed and used in 1930–1950. Psychosurgery involved shocking the patient into a coma then the surgeon had to hammer a tool similar to an ice pick into the socket of the eye to detach the nerves which joined the frontal lobes to the centres in the brain which controlled emotions. The aim was to manage the patient's aggressive feelings.

Because of its low costs and the short time it took to complete the procedure, the treatment spread widely; though at first, it appeared to be successful. In later years, the patients who had undergone the procedure were not able to put a restraint on their impulses. The patients also became shallow and calm in an unnatural way and exhibited no feelings whatsoever.

The procedure was abandoned with the introduction of psychoactive drugs. Lithium, one of the drugs, was launched in 1949. Later in the 1950s, more drugs were introduced, which helped in controlling the symptoms of psychosis, though they did not cure the condition. In 1952, France discovered chlorpromazine, and Valium was later discovered in the 1960s, and it became the tranquilliser that is most prescribed in the world. In 1987, Prozac was introduced, and it became the most prescribed antidepressant in the world (Porter, 2002).

The introduction of drugs which were psychoactive contributed largely to the end of mental hospitals which had been established in the 1960s. Facilities which were based in the community became more preferred as opposed to the psychiatric hospitals. Having these facilities became a short-lived plan since those released from the mental hospitals were unable to live without depending on others. The outcome was that these individuals had no homes to live in since there was not enough housing, and they did not receive any care after leaving the psychiatric hospitals.

The psychotropic drugs have also made people affected by mental illness become incapable of addressing issues regarding their mental well-being. The shame associated with mental illnesses has made many patients resort to self-treatment by the use of only psychotropic medicine to hide their disorder from their family and friends.

In modern times, there are still people who believe that mental illness is a result of supernatural happenings. These people end up consulting traditional doctors or healers first in search of a cure. It is only when they do not receive cure from the traditional healers that they resort to the medical profession. An example is Nigeria where people affected by mental illness accepted admission in the asylums after the traditional healers were unable to help them (Sadowsky, 2007).

In the modern society, mental illness seems to be a growing problem, especially among young people. In the society today, the causes of mental illness are thought to be genetic or a result of the influence from the environment the person lives. Those affected by mental illness are no longer being taken to institutions unless they portray behaviour that shows they can harm themselves or others. The moves against institutionalising the individuals affected by mental illness have had some drawbacks; the ill individuals have ended up in prison or become homeless since few people are willing to take care of them. The result has been the introduction of different methods of treating those affected by mental illness. One example is the assertive community treatment which comprises specialists, nurses, social workers, and psychiatrists who offer services to those who are mentally ill but are either not willing or cannot go to a doctor. The services are usually offered in the sick person's home environment. Despite the different treatment options that have been offered, those affected by mental illness are still ostracised and stigmatised in the society. An example is when a person acts or behaves differently, they tend to be termed as being affected by mental illness. Also, there are people still in the modern times who believe that mental illnesses are non-existent.

Signs of Mental Illness

Different mental illnesses have different signs and symptoms, but the most common ones include noticeable changes in a person's personality and becoming unable to handle challenges and activities in their daily life. Another sign indicating the presence of a mental illness is extreme fear and anxiety, which can be a sign of anxiety disorder. When an individual has extended periods of depression, this can be an indication of a mental illness. Also, when an individual has moods which are very high and later become very low, it can be a sign of bipolar disorder. People who have mental illness at times tend to become extremely angry, hostile, or violent. When one or more of these symptoms are present, the person or their family should seek medical help from qualified health personnel.

Causes of Mental Illness

There are various factors which cause mental illness. They include biological, environmental, and psychological.

Biological Factors

A biological factor is *heredity*. This is where the illness runs in a particular family and is passed from one generation to another. The mental illness is usually passed through genes which are abnormal. For people who have a genetic susceptibility and encounter stress, abuse, or trauma, this can act as a trigger for the illness. Another biological factor that leads to mental illness is when a person has deformities or injuries in some parts of the brain. Prenatal injury during the early development of the brain for a foetus when it's still in its mother's womb can also cause mental illness. The foetal damage can be a result of the environment or the surrounding which the mother lives. In case the mother is exposed to stress, trauma, lack of enough food, and infections, all these can cause prenatal injuries. The damage which arises during birth can result in autism spectrum disorder among other mental illnesses.

Infections can also cause mental illnesses. An example of one mental illness caused by infections is the paediatric autoimmune neuropsychiatric disorder (PANDA) which is linked to bacteria and can lead to mental illness in children. One of the mental illnesses caused by PANDA is the obsessive-compulsive disorder.

Environmental Factors

Environmental factors refer to the stresses which an individual has to deal with on a daily basis. The stresses can include financial challenges, having a dysfunctional family, substance and drug abuse, poverty, poor relationships, low self-esteem among others. Other environmental factors that can lead to mental illness are violence, loneliness, the death of a close person, homelessness, unemployment, trauma either as a child or as an adult, and experience of being a crime victim. Life experiences (an example is when abuse occurs to either a child or an adult; the abuse can be sexual, emotional or even physical) can trigger mental illness. When these experiences cumulate over an extended period, they can result in a mental illness. Children who have experienced poor parenting from their parents or caretakers by being neglected or mistreated as children are at a risk of getting depression.

Issues related to relationships can lead to mental illness; for instance, the divorce of parents can result in the child developing depression or other mental disorders, either as a child or later as an adult. Dysfunctional families have also been linked to people from these families developing various types of mental illness. When a person's self-esteem is either too low or too high, it can lead to mental illness. The reason is that the individual may not be able to fit in the society, and they may become a bully, which further leads to feelings of anger, violence, and later, depression.

There exists a correlation between poverty and mental illness. People whose economic status is low are at a higher risk of developing mental illness compared to those whose economic and social status is high. The reason is because those whose economic status is low have to deal with stressors related to economic issues. The stressors can be lack of housing which is affordable to them and unemployment. Some of these people may end up abusing substances or drugs, which eventually leads to mental disorders. Toxins, such as lead, can also lead to mental illness to those living in this toxic environment. Drug and substance abuse can result in mental illness. An example is the use of alcohol, which can cause depression, and amphetamines, which can cause paranoia and anxiety.

Psychological Factors

Some of the psychological factors which can give rise to mental illness are abuse, whether emotional, physical, or sexual; the loss of a close person, either a friend or a family member; and the inability to relate with other people. People respond differently to life stresses; what breaks one individual may have little or no effect on another person. Some individuals are emotionally detached; in some instances, they may become neurotic.

The Brain and Mental Illness

The presence of a mental illness in a person is usually an indication that the brain has some problems. The brain is a complex organ; it comprises 2 per cent of the total body weight. The consumption of oxygen and energy by the brain is 20 per cent of the total oxygen used by a person. The brain controls what a human being does on a daily basis, which includes their movement and the regulation of body processes which are involuntary, such as breathing. The fundamental working unit of the brain is the neuron. A cell membrane surrounds a neuron which divides the cell contents which are inside from the environment which surrounds it. The small spaces between the neurons are referred to as synapses; they help in the transmission of information between the neurons.

A neuron has three regions, namely, dendrites, axon, and cell body. The cell body contains the cell organelles, the nucleus, and the cytoplasm. The DNA, the information required for cell growth and repair, are contained in the nucleus. The substance which occupies or fills the cell is referred to as the cytoplasm. The dendrites are the neuron's contact points in getting and transmitting the electrical and chemical signals or impulses from other neurons. The axon helps in sending impulses to a different nerve cell. The neuron contains processes referred to as dendrites which get messages or information. The other units called axon sends signals to a different neuron. The dendrite is smaller compared to the axon which can be as long as one metre.

Electrical signals are used in communication by the neurons; the electrical signals carry information from the cell body of the neuron to the axon's final point. In establishing whether a person has mental illness or not, the medical professionals base their treatment on the individual's symptoms only. On the other hand, the scientists involved in research have an aim of wanting to study the person's brain changes, both chemically and structurally, to establish whether one has mental illness or not.

The scientists use biochemical or molecular techniques, depending on the questions which they intend to ask the patient. This is because the experts believe that the cause of mental illness is poor communication in the brain. Imaging techniques enable the scientists to study the brain; one of the techniques that have been used widely is the positron emission topography, whose acronym is PET. The method is used while the individual is awake; this helps to analyse the link between the physiological and behavioural effects and the brain activity's changes. A computer is used to reassemble pictures from the PET scan. This technique can identify regions of the brain where the neurons are more active compared to other regions. By the use of glucose which is radio-labelled, those areas of the brain which are most active can be identified through their response to a particular stimulus, the reason being neurons which are active in comparison to those which are inactive metabolise more glucose.

On the PET scan, neurons which are active release additional number of positrons which displays on the scan either a yellow or red, and the inactive neurons show a purple or a blue on the scan. Scientists use this method to establish how the brain activity of a patient is affected by mental illnesses before and after treatment.

There are other techniques used by research scientists to identify how the brain changes because of mental illnesses. These other techniques include magnetic resonance imaging (MRI) which is used to establish changes of a structural nature in the brain. The MRI makes use of magnetic fields to help in taking pictures of the structure of the brain. The method helps in showing spaces which are in the brain, which are referred to as ventricles. They are bigger in people having schizophrenia compared to individuals who do not have the condition.

Research scientists also make use of magneto encephalography (MEG) in establishing particular patterns of the brain to foretell the people that can respond to fast-acting antidepressant drugs. By doing this, trial and error is avoided in administering drugs to people suffering from depression by knowing who will respond to the rapid-acting antidepressants.

In addition, recent evidence has indicated that mesenchymal stem cells (MSCs) can be an effective alternative therapy for patients with mental illness. This can be attributed to the fact that treatment through this method has shown neurogenerative and neuroprotective effects, both of which are essential for the treatment of mental illness (Choi et al., 2014). Choi et al. (2014) mainly argued that autologous adipose tissue-derived mesenchymal stem cells transplantation can be an effective treatment as carried out by them on a patient with symptoms of neurological diseases to produce useful results. Choi et al. (2014) concluded that the treatment of a progressive supranuclear palsy patient with the use of this method was completely safe and would help in delaying the progression of neurological deficits through the functional improvement achievement.

Neurotransmitters and Mental Illness

Whatever a person does is mostly based on the communication that happens between neurons (Reuter, 1983). Neurotransmitters help in relaying messages between the neurons. When the message or signal reaches the neuron's end, the neurotransmitter pours into space or gap and crosses it. The storage of the neurotransmitters is the synapse. Neurotransmitters can fail to function normally because of the lack of sufficient transmitters, having more neurotransmitters than needed and the malabsorption of the neurotransmitters. When this communication fails, mental illness occurs. Some of the mental illnesses caused by poor communication between the neurons are depression and tremors. There are several types of neurotransmitters, which include serotonin, dopamine, glutamate among others.

Serotonin, which is mostly found in the intestine, helps in the control of functions, such as appetite, sleep, and the person's mood. People suffering from depression usually suffer from low serotonin levels in their brains. Dopamine helps in the movement control and assists in information flow to the forepart of the brain, which is connected to one's emotions and thoughts. When dopamine levels are too low, it can result in schizophrenia. Glutamate, which is a common type of neurotransmitter, helps in the transmission of excitement; it also aids in memory and learning. The wrong use of glutamate can be connected to several mental illnesses or disorders, which include depression, schizophrenia, and obsessive-compulsive disorder.

How Neurotransmitters Influences the Mind

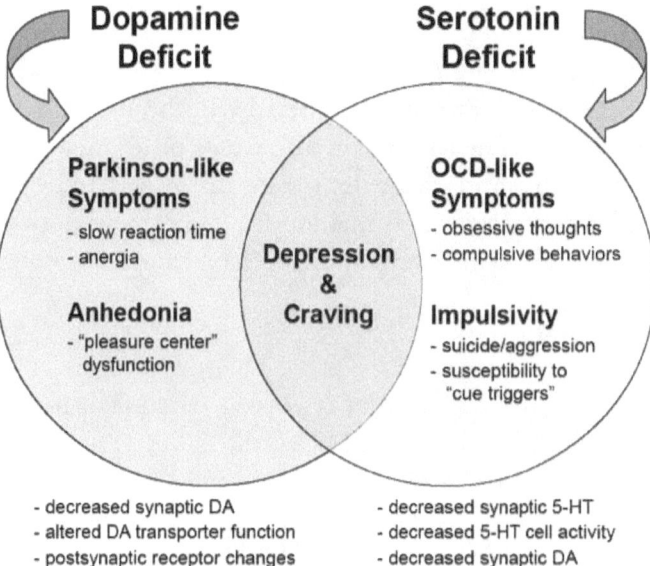

Types of Mental Illnesses

In the society today, there are many mental illnesses or disorders. Examples are anxiety disorders, bipolar disorder, obsessive-compulsive disorder, depression, drug-induced psychosis, and schizophrenia among others.

Anxiety Disorders

Anxiety is normal in the day-to-day life of people, but when a person has anxiety or fear all the time, this can no longer be termed as normal anxiety but as a disorder. Anxiety disorder is a mental illness where a person experiences emotions of fear and anxiety which are continuous and which disrupts the person's daily activities and way of life.

Symptoms

These feelings can result in symptoms which are physical, such as the person begins to shake and have an increase in heart rate. Anxiety disorders can be caused by both environmental and hereditary factors. The illness can also cause other mental illnesses, such as personality and major depressive disorder. Anxiety disorder has several categories, which include the general anxiety disorder, panic disorder, social and separation anxiety disorders among others.

General Anxiety

The general anxiety disorder is where a person has no particular reason for being anxious (Spitzer et al., 2006). The people most affected are the older adults; the causes can be either a substance abuse or a medical problem. The symptoms can include the person becoming restless and irritable, having problems in their concentration, and at times, their mind going blank. A person with general anxiety can also have problems with their sleep and is subject to getting tired easily.

Panic Disorder

Panic disorder is where the affected person has violent attacks for a short period. The person tends to shake, trembles, becomes breathless, and becomes confused. The triggers of these attacks can include stress or fear. The person may also feel that they are out of control in their lives and tend to worry about the next panic attack, and they may tend to avoid the places where they experienced the panic attack.

Social Anxiety/Phobia

Social anxiety disorder is characterised by a person avoiding publicity which is negative, embarrassing or publicly humiliating (Beidel & Turner, 2007). Those who experience this type of disorder tend to fear to speak publicly. The symptoms which the person experiences can include sweating, feeling self-conscious while addressing people, and having difficulty in speaking. The person with social phobia can worry for months, weeks, or days before the event; they may tend to avoid places where there are people or social gatherings.

A Cognitive Model of Social Phobia

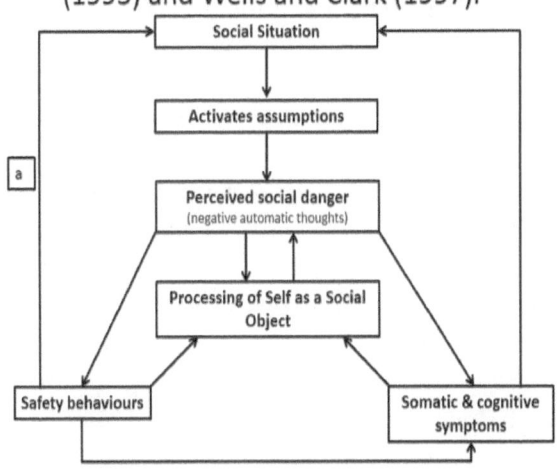

Cognitive model of social phobia (Clarks and Wells (1995) and Wells and Clark (1997).

Wells, A., 1997. Cognitive Therapy of Anxiety Disorders: A Practice Manual and Conceptual Guide. Chichester: John Wiley & Sons Ltd.

Separation Phobia/Anxiety

Separation anxiety refers to an individual having an extreme fear of being separated from people or a particular place. Children are the most affected by this type of anxiety. To prevent this, children should get treatment early.

This kind of fear tends to occur mostly when the individual is experiencing stress. Since they occur in conjunction with other mental illnesses, the diagnosis should be made early. Treatment can include changes in the person's lifestyle; for example, the person should have a regular sleep pattern, and the individual who smokes should stop the habit.

Anxiety Disorders Treatment Methods

Medication

In offering treatment, medication can also be used to relieve the symptoms of anxiety but not to cure the disorder. Most of the medications or drugs need to be taken on a regular basis since sometimes symptoms recur when the medication is stopped. Antidepressant medications are also used in treating anxiety disorder. The patient should be made aware of the side effects of these drugs, which include nausea, problems in sleeping, and headaches. There are also drugs which help in reducing anxiety. An example is the benzodiazepines, which is used for treating general anxiety.

Therapy

Psychotherapy is another form of treatment, where the patient talks about their fears. It is useful in treating anxiety disorders. Cognitive behavioural therapy has been proven the most useful in treating anxiety disorders. It involves the identification of thoughts which are unhelpful in the patients and comes up with ways of neutralising these thoughts. Exposure therapy is also helpful; here, the patient is helped to use relaxation techniques to get rid of the anxieties and fears.

Techniques for Managing Stress

Techniques, such as meditation and aerobic exercises, can assist in making a person affected by an anxiety disorder to relax. The individual gets advice on how to reduce their intake of illegal drugs and caffeine which may cause the condition to worsen. The involvement of the patient's family and friends is also helpful in their recovery process.

Prevention and Management of Anxiety Disorders

There are various strategies and prevention methods which can help a person who is experiencing anxiety disorders. Some of the strategies include looking for help early enough from a mental health professional. Avoidance of substance and alcohol abuse can also assist in reducing the fears and anxieties which the individual may be experiencing. Exercise can also help in reducing anxiety. The reason is that the person during exercise pays more attention to the sensations they are experiencing and pays little attention to anxious thoughts and feelings.

Meditation helps in relaxation. This helps the person in getting rid of the anxious and fearful thoughts and feelings. Sleep deprivation can cause worry and anxiety. The person experiencing anxiety disorder should try to sleep for at least seven hours daily. The doctor can also administer drugs which may help in restoring the sleep pattern. Changing the thought pattern where the individual with the anxiety disorder focuses more on positive thinking can also help in reducing anxiety.

Bipolar Disorder

This is a mental disorder where a patient has durations or intervals where they are depressed and, at times, they are delighted. *Mania* is when the person affected by mental illness experiences extreme elation or excitement. During this duration, the person experiences a feeling of unusual energy, happiness, or irritability. The individual may not sleep because of the high energy they are experiencing. On the other hand, when the patient is experiencing depression, they begin to look at life negatively, and they tend to cry a lot. Because of the different feelings that the person has on a day-to-day basis, the rate of those who take away their lives through suicide is high as the person is not in control of their emotions.

The causes of bipolar disorder can be either hereditary or a result of the environment that the individual grew up or lives. The environmental aspects include abuse when one was a child and stress which is long-term. Bipolar is classified into either bipolar 1 or 11, depending on the number of manic occurrences that the individual has encountered. Research has shown that bipolar disorder symptoms usually start at the age of twenty-five. Both men and women seem to be affected in equal measures. A person suffering from bipolar disorder often exhibits the following symptoms: manic, hypomanic, and depressive occurrences or episodes.

Manic Attack/Episode

This is a duration which lasts for at least one week, where the individual experiences high levels of irritability or moods which are elevated. When the manic episodes begin, the person may lack sleep or have disturbances in their sleep pattern. The person also tends to speak fast, has their attention level being low, and is easily agitated. The individual is also unable to socialise or even work. If left untreated, manic episodes can result in psychosis.

Hypomanic Attack/Episode

This is a mania that is light or mild. Some of its symptoms, which may last for weeks or months, include a reduced desire for sleep. The patient may not remember the outcome of their actions on those people around them. This condition is not as severe as the manic disorder; the individual can still socialise. It is in very few instances that this situation develops to an advanced manic disorder.

Depressive Attack/Episode

A patient with bipolar disorder experiences continuous feelings of anger, sadness, and lack of interest in activities that the individual enjoyed before; they also feel irritable. The patient may either sleep a lot or not sleep at all; there are also significant changes in their weight. In a case where the depressive disorder becomes severe, the sick person may start exhibiting psychotic symptoms. The symptoms can include hallucinations and delusions. In case this illness is left untreated, it can result in suicide.

Diagnosis of Bipolar Disorder

The diagnosis of this order is usually conducted during adolescence or when the person is in their early adulthood. Any abnormal behaviour reported by the person or their family, friends, and co-workers are taken into consideration. There are various tools used in diagnosing bipolar disorder, which include the *Diagnostic and Statistical Manual of Mental Disorders*, fifth edition (DSM-5), by the American Psychiatric Association.

Bipolar Disorder Treatment Methods

Psychotherapy

The treatment of bipolar disorder can involve the use of psychotherapy, which aim is to reduce the critical symptoms. This treatment can also help the patient on ways to identify the situations which trigger the attack. During therapy, the individual is also taught on how to practice the aspects that can help them manage the condition or on the ways in which they can completely alleviate the symptoms.

Medication

Medication is also used in treating bipolar disorder; one of the most commonly administered drugs is lithium, which helps in the treatment of manic and depressive attacks (American Psychiatric Association, 2002). To help in stabilising the moods of the patients suffering from bipolar disorder, anticonvulsant drugs are given. In the prevention of relapses in the patient, Olanzapine drug is usually prescribed.

The patient is expected to comply with the medication given to reduce the relapse rate and to be able to live a normal life. Recognising the disorder early enough helps in reducing the severity of the illness and one's response rate to treatment. One of the drugs which can be utilised is the selective serotonin reuptake inhibitor (SSRI) for those suffering from depression as it helps in increasing the serotonin level in their brain.

Management of Bipolar Disorder

For the individuals who have been diagnosed with bipolar disorder, it is necessary to learn on how to manage or control the disorder. There are several things which can help in the management of bipolar disorder, among them being the insurance that they take their medication as prescribed by the doctor and the maintenance of a daily routine where they do things at specific times, which can help reduce stress. Also, getting enough sleep for the person with bipolar disorder can assist in controlling the depressive or manic episodes.

The person should avoid alcohol and substance abuse. The reason is that alcohol can play havoc with one's sleep; alcohol can also hinder the effectiveness of the medicine the patient is taking. The individual should reduce stress to avoid the manic or depressive episodes. The person should also learn about the early symptoms of the attack and enlighten those around them. This will help when in case the individual has a manic attack, the family can seek for treatment instantly since they are aware of the symptoms.

Drug-Induced Psychosis

Psychosis is a state of mind that is altered, where the person affected has a break from reality. The person experiences hallucinations or delusions. Psychosis can occur as a result of alcohol or substance abuse. Drug- or substance-induced psychosis is a psychosis which is linked to the abuse of drugs. There have been a lot of discussions concerning the relationship which exists between the use of drugs and psychosis. It is hard at times to establish whether psychosis which is induced through drugs has been caused by a person self-medicating or abusing drugs because of other factors not related to any illness.

When there is drug abuse or intoxicants for an extended period, this can lead to drug abuse psychosis. In some instances, when the effect of the drug diminishes, the psychosis may cease. There are times when psychosis may be a result of withdrawal symptoms of either alcohol or drugs on a person who has been dependent on the drugs and alcohol. This kind of psychosis disappears when the withdrawal symptoms are over. There is a high rate of psychosis which is drug-induced for those people who abuse drugs and who have a predisposition for mental illnesses.

Drugs/Stimulants That Can Cause Drug-Induced Psychosis

There are various drugs or stimulants which cause different psychotic signs. Some of the stimulants include cocaine and amphetamine, whose abuse cause paranoia; problems with memory; hallucinations, both visual and auditory (Hurlbut, 1991). Users of cocaine usually exhibit symptoms of delusions which are related to persecution and hallucinations. The symptoms can continue for an extended period even after one ceases using the drug. The person using these stimulants tends to become aggressive, violent, and hostile. Abuse of depressants, such as marijuana, alcohol, and benzodiazepines, causes hallucinations, delirium, ringing in the ears, disorientation, and confusion mentally. The use of cannabis by a person can result in schizophrenia. The person may start to experience anxiety and perceptions which are distorted. The individual's behaviour becomes violent; they start experiencing hallucinations, and their sense of time and space become distorted. Methamphetamine can result in one becoming paranoid, hallucinating, and beginning to hear voices. One type of hallucination which comes as a result of using methamphetamine is having the feeling of crawling bugs on the skin.

Hallucinogens, which include ketamine, peyote, ecstasy, LSD, and PCD, results into reality alteration, loss of memory, and delusions in the person who uses them. The use of ecstasy, which is a recreational drug, can cause behaviours which are antisocial and panic attacks. Users of ketamine, which is a prescription medicine, end up having symptoms that are similar to psychosis. An example is a person starting to experiencing delusions, having confused thoughts, and the speech becoming incoherent. LCD and PCP use can also result in psychotic-like symptoms, but once the individual ceases to use the drugs, the symptoms disappear.

Some of the people that use psychosis which is drug-induced take alcohol to handle the symptoms. This is self-medication which is not right since at times, this can make the symptoms worse. The result can be a cycle, where the individual becomes independent on both drugs and alcohol.

Causes of Psychosis

There are various causes of psychosis which can include history of the family and experiences that one has in life; an example is stress, trauma, or sickness. Abuse of drug and alcohol also causes psychosis.

Symptoms/Signs of Psychosis

Some of the symptoms which indicate that a person has psychosis include having thoughts which are disorganised and having delusions which means beliefs that are false involving an individual's perception, where the person tends to believe that they have supernatural powers. Some of the feelings that can indicate the presence of psychosis are lacking interest in day-to-day activities and getting easily agitated and confused.

A person with psychosis can also experience problems in conversations, that is, they are unable to keep track of what they are saying. The individual may be unable to remember things, become easily angered, and not be aware of their surroundings. Other symptoms of psychosis include having unseemly behaviour; an example is acting in a silly manner.

Treatment Methods for Psychosis

There are various treatments which are used for patients who have psychosis which is a result of substance abuse. The treatment depends on various factors, among them being the type of substance used, the severity of the disorder, and the willingness of the individual to change. Also, the environment where the person seeking treatment lives has a significant influence on the kind of treatment suitable to them.

The treatment has various objectives; one of them is to stop the person from substance abuse. For the long-term treatment, the objective is to help the person reduce the number of times that they abuse the drugs or substance. The individual should participate in the recovery process; this may have a great impact on the individual, reducing their intake of the substances. The treatment should also aim at helping the individual to repair any damage caused to or by the person during the period in which they were abusing drugs. The treatment given depends on the cost, the duration which the treatment will take place, and whether the person is an inpatient or outpatient.

Medication

Medication can be used in the treatment of drug-induced psychosis. Medication can either be antidepressant or antipsychotic. Some of the antipsychotic medicines which are used for treatment include chlorpromazine, fluphenazine, perphenazine, paliperidone, lurasidone among others. Some of the medications used have a side effect which the user should be made aware of by the doctor. The physician's instructions are necessary for the patient to follow when they are taking the medication. In cases when the individual who has psychotic symptoms is using either alcohol or drugs, it is necessary to make the doctor aware since these can interfere with the effectiveness of the medication.

Medication is also given for those experiencing withdrawal symptoms. The medicine given is usually in the same class of pharmacology where there is the replacement of the substance which the patient was abusing with medication in the same class pharmacologically.

Psychosocial Treatment

The purpose of this treatment is to help the patient learn how to manage stress and bring about changes in their behaviours. The patient is taught how to handle anxiety and is given training on relaxation and social skills. In the situation where the patient is dependent on alcohol, they are advised to join alcohol programmes to be able to deal with the dependence. In case there is a need to see a psychologist, the patient is referred to one. The treatment can also include the family members of the individual; this helps when the psychotic symptoms have caused conflict within the family. Programmes to control relapse are necessary for attaining long-term solutions for the individual.

Cognitive Behavioural Therapy

Cognitive behavioural therapy is helpful in the management of moods in depression and anxiety. The individual, because of dependence on drugs, may not be able to relate well with the community that they live in; the therapy will help in training the patient on social skills. The cognitive behavioural therapy will help the individual avoid consumption of illegal substance and self-medicating.

Outpatient and Inpatient Services

People who have abused cocaine or some substances together can benefit from inpatient services. Outpatient clinics are usually for individuals whose psychotic disorder is a result of being primary users of nicotine and marijuana.

Detoxification

Drug-induced psychosis can benefit from detoxification which is monitored by a health professional. The process is usually done in a hospital setup or a rehabilitation centre.

Obsessive-Compulsive Disorder

This is a mental illness or disorder where the person feels the need to repeatedly check on things, do some procedures, or have some thoughts repeatedly. The individual who has this kind of illness is unable to control their thoughts for long periods. The activities that these people engage in repeatedly are washing of their hands and confirming if the doors are locked. The individual performs these activities to the extent that their daily life is affected negatively. The disorder is related to anxiety disorders.

Symptoms of Obsessive-Compulsive Disorder

The disorder has many symptoms; some of the most common ones are having unwelcomed or undesirable thoughts repeatedly (Leckman et al., 1997). The individual has a fear of getting contamination; thus, they frequently wash their hands or clean their house for hours. For some people, they continually think about sex-related issues; the thoughts may be a taboo. Also, the person may have pictures or images where they see themselves hurting other people or being harmed by others. Obsessive-compulsive disorder can cause the affected person to repeatedly check or count things. An example is when the affected person is counting when they are climbing the stairs, where the person believes a certain number is a bad omen; to avoid the omen, the person will avoid stepping on that particular stair. The individual may also have an obsession of arranging things to face a particular direction.

Other symptoms of the disorder are being constantly anxious and being very emotional. The individual can also pick on their skin continuously. They can repeatedly check whether doors or ovens are locked; this can be a result of the individual feeling afraid or irresponsible, thus seeing the need to check on things many times. Another symptom of the obsessive-compulsive disorder is the tendency to analyse the relationships with friends and family; they may get preoccupied with an innocent gesture or remark made by their friends or family. Because the person consumes most of their time on doing things repeatedly, they may be unable to perform their daily activities. Their sleep patterns are disturbed; they tend to sleep for short periods only. People with obsessive-compulsive disorder can also develop other conditions which include bipolar disorder, anxiety disorder, major depressive disorder among others.

The Causes of Obsessive-Compulsive Disorder

One of the causes of obsessive-compulsive disorder is hereditary or genetic. Identical twins are more prone to this illness in comparison to twins who are not identical. Lack of the serotonin chemical in the brain can cause the disorder. Another factor which has been seen to influence the occurrence of the disorder is an individual's experiences in life. Some of the experiences include trauma or abuse either as a child or as an adult. In coping with the fear and anxiety that came as a result of the abuse, the child may have learned obsessive or compulsive behaviours.

Another personal experience that can bring about obsessive-compulsive disorder is learning the compulsive behaviours from one's parents; in case the parents had anxieties or some obsessive behaviour, the child may end up picking the behaviour. Obsessive-compulsive disorder can be caused by beliefs which are dysfunctional. An example of some of these thoughts is when a person fears that people want to push them out of a moving vehicle. The person may end becoming anxious and act in a way to prevent this from happening.

Diagnosis of Obsessive-Compulsive Disorder

The diagnosis of obsessive-compulsive disorder is usually made by a professional in mental health, who can either be a psychiatrist, psychologist, or doctor who has the training in dealing with mental issues. The instrument mostly used is the structured clinical interview to examine whether the patient has symptoms indicating the existence of the disorder. The structured clinical interview consists of questions of a standard nature so that all patients can undergo the same kind of interview. The questions asked relate to the patient's medical and family history, which will include the patient's age and general health, the severity of the symptoms, the duration which the patient has experienced the symptom, and any other illness that the patient may have. The type of childhood that the patient had can contribute to them having obsessive-compulsive disorder, so the professional should ask questions along this line.

The mental health professional may question the patient on whether the symptoms came as a result of any illness to determine whether there is any relationship between the disorder and the sickness. The mental professional can ask the patient the effect the symptoms have had on their daily life and the duration that the patient has had the symptoms.

Treatment for Obsessive-Compulsive Disorder

Therapy

One of the treatments for the illness is giving therapy to the patient. The cognitive behavioural therapy is useful; here, the patient talks about how they think, believe, and view various issues which affect their conduct and feelings. One type of cognitive behavioural therapy is the exposure and response prevention (ERP), where the patient is taught on how to manage and control their compulsions and obsessions. The mental health professional or therapist puts the patient in an environment where they get anxious; the patient is taught to tolerate the anxiety rather than become compulsive. The purpose of ERP is to help the patient realise that the anxious and uncomfortable feelings eventually disappear. As the therapy continues, the patient recognises that the obsessions they have been having do not culminate in anxiety as before.

Medication

There are various medications which can help in treating obsessive-compulsive disorder; they include antidepressants and tranquillisers which are given in cases of severe anxiety. The antidepressants include selective serotonin reuptake inhibitors (SSRI), which include fluoxetine, fluvoxamine, and citalopram. In the case where the patient is not responsive to SSRI, the health professional can prescribe clomipramine. Beta-blockers are prescribed once in a while in the treatment of symptoms of anxiety which are physical. The side effect of clomipramine is feeling sleepy, blood pressure dropping when waking up from sitting down. The patient also experiences a dry mouth and has difficulty urinating.

Psychosurgery

This kind of treatment helps in bringing relief to the symptoms which a patient who has the obsessive-compulsive disorder experiences. This is usually done to patients who do not respond to medication or therapy. The treatment involves four types of surgery. The first surgery is where there is the drilling of the skull and the anterior cingulate cortex which a region in the brain is burnt with a probe which is hot. Only 50 per cent of the patients who underwent this kind of surgery benefit. The second type of surgery is where doctors operate on the anterior lobe of the inner capsule; the surgery has helped 50 to 60 per cent of patients with obsessive-compulsive disorder.

The third type of surgery for patients with obsessive-compulsive disorder is termed as gamma knife; through this procedure, there is the penetration of the skull, but the skull is not opened. The method is beneficial when used once, but when used for more than once, it becomes harmful to the brain tissue. The fourth procedure is psychosurgery or the deep brain stimulation (DBS); here, there is the opening of the skull while preserving the tissues in the brain. DBS makes use of a generator that uses power and works the same way as a pacemaker.

Therapy

There are various therapies available for patients with obsessive-compulsive disorder; some of the therapies are for a short duration, while others are for an extended period. In most cases, during treatment, the patient's family is involved.

Centres for Obsessive-Compulsive Disorder Patients

Some patients do not respond to either medicine or therapy, and they have to be taken to centres where they are taken care of as inpatients. The centres use both therapy and psychopharmacological methods in treating these patients. Most of these centres research and give provision for treatment which is tailored to a particular patient.

Rehabilitation Centres for Outpatients

There are also outpatient facilities which cater for patients with obsessive-compulsive disorder. The staffs in these institutions or centres are committed to the welfare of the patients. During the rehabilitation process, both the patient and their family are involved.

In these centres, research is conducted to help in discovering better and advanced methods to use in the patient's treatment and recovery.

Management of Obsessive-Compulsive Disorder

The person experiencing obsessive-compulsive disorder can learn on how to manage it; some of the things that the individual can do are to confront their fears and not to avoid it. The individual can expose themself to the triggers of the disorder and try to avoid the desire to look for relief though the use of a compulsive behaviour. Constant exposure to compulsive and obsessive triggers helps the person with the illness have less anxiety. The person can also focus their thoughts on other things or engage in other activities which deviate their mind from the compulsive behaviour. Some of the activities that the individual can focus on include exercising, reading, knitting, or doing something which they enjoy; this will help them not to dwell on obsessive thoughts.

The individual experiencing the obsessive and compulsive thoughts should be able to foresee or predict the thoughts beforehand. An example is if the person has an obsession about closing the door many times, they can close the door and then create a mental picture where they tell themselves that the door is locked. In case the desire to check if the door has been closed comes in their mind, they should tell themselves that the thought is not true but just an obsession. Writing can also help in the management of obsessive-compulsive disorder symptoms; writing is harder than thinking, and this can make the compulsive thoughts to vanish.

Techniques for relaxation can also help the individual in controlling the obsessive thoughts, sleeping as much as possible can also assist in controlling anxious thoughts. Support groups are helpful in managing obsessive-compulsive disorders since the individual can talk about their fears which reduce their power. By joining a support group for people with obsessive-compulsive disorder, the person is able to share their experiences with people having the same challenges. The person should also avoid isolation since isolation increases the obsessive-compulsive disorder symptoms.

Schizophrenia

This is a mental illness or disorder which affects someone's thoughts, feelings, and actions. The person's behaviour is usually abnormal, and they do not understand reality. Men exhibit symptoms related to schizophrenia early in life in comparison to women. Children rarely have schizophrenia. Symptoms of schizophrenia start showing between the ages of sixteen to thirty years. Schizophrenia can lead to disability (Eaton et al., 2012).

Symptoms of Schizophrenia

A person who has schizophrenia usually has hallucinations, where they hear voices or start to see things that do not exist. Another symptom is having delusions where the individual tends to believe things which have no basis in reality (Consortium, 2009). Some examples include the person thinking that someone is out to harm them or that people are talking about them and that a major disaster is about to occur. This mental disorder also causes the thoughts and speech of the affected individual to have no organisation. A question can be asked to the person, and the reply given may not relate to the question asked, or it may have no meaning.

The person may also exhibit signs of extreme disorganisation; they may act like a child or suddenly develop agitation. They can refuse to accept instructions given, have movements which they are not able to control, and at times, have no response emotionally. Teenagers can have signs that indicate the existence of schizophrenia; they include withdrawing from friends and family, performance at school dropping, becoming easily irritable, and lacking in motivation. Teenagers may have fewer delusions and more hallucinations in comparison to adults.

Positive Symptoms

Symptoms of schizophrenia can either be positive or negative. The positive signs are those which people affected by schizophrenia usually experience, but others may not be experiencing them. The positive signs include hallucinations, delusions, and thoughts with no organisation, which are common, but some people may not experience them.

Negative Symptoms

These symptoms indicate lack of normal emotional reactions; the person with the symptoms is usually not responsive to the medicine given. Some of these emotions which are regarded as flat are being unable to experience pleasure, emotions being absent, having no desire to have any relationship, reducing speech. The negative symptoms cause the life quality to be poor.

The Causes of Schizophrenia

Hereditary/Genetic Factors

Genes have a significant influence in a person developing schizophrenia, where parents or one parent has schizophrenia; there is a high likelihood of passing the same to their children. In cases where there are identical twins, if one of them develops schizophrenia, there is a high chance that the other twin will develop the illness.

Schizophrenia and Brain Development

The brain structure of people who have schizophrenia is different from those who are healthy; this indicates that brain disorder can cause schizophrenia. Neurotransmitters have a connection to schizophrenia; alteration in the levels of dopamine and serotonins, which are two types of transmitters, can cause schizophrenia.

Environmental Factors

Some viral infections can lead to schizophrenia, in particular, for the unborn children. Lack of right nutrition for a pregnant woman for the first six months can cause the foetus to develop this mental disorder. Trauma experienced during an individual's childhood, for example, the parents' dying when the person was still a child, can also raise the risk of mental illness. The stressors of life can also cause schizophrenia; some of these stressors are getting bereaved, having a divorce, ending a relationship among others.

Substance Abuse

Drug abuse and alcohol consumption are linked to schizophrenia. Some of the drugs include cocaine and marijuana; they increase the chances of developing schizophrenia, particularly for those people who are prone or susceptible to the illness. The younger the person is while starting to abuse drugs, the riskier it is for them to develop schizophrenia.

Developmental Factors

There are factors related to the development process of a child which can cause them to develop schizophrenia. Some of these factors include infections, the mother experiencing malnutrition during the growth of the foetus, and lack of oxygen during birth. Also, infections that occur during delivery can also cause this disorder.

Diagnosis of Schizophrenia

The diagnosis is made when symptoms which indicate the presence of schizophrenia are present. The symptoms may include hallucinations, delusions, random thoughts, or negative symptoms among others. Neurological examination is done to establish whether the person has schizophrenia or other mental illnesses. The reason is because some symptoms of schizophrenia are similar to those of other mental disorders, such as the personality and social anxiety disorders.

Diagnosis is made after the patient experiences symptoms related to schizophrenia for more than one month but not exceeding six months. There should be the indication that dysfunction has occurred in the person's social and career life. When the symptoms are for a period less than one month, the diagnosis usually is a psychotic disorder which is for a short time. The American Psychiatric Association or the *Diagnostic and Statistical Manual of Mental Disorders*

(*DSM-5*) are mostly used in the diagnosis of schizophrenia. The tests use the experiences that the patient has had and any abnormal behaviour that may have been reported concerning the patient.

Treatment and Management of Schizophrenia

Though there is no known cure for schizophrenia, the illness can be controlled and treated. The treatment involves contribution from both medicine and psychology. The patient should have medical care in other areas; an example is if the patient has diabetes, then the medical personnel should ensure the patient gets treatment. There are various treatments for schizophrenia. They include antipsychotic medicine and psychosocial treatment. Treatment is usually given for outpatients, but at times, patients who have had issues of substance abuse and an illness which is physical can be taken as inpatients in the hospital for a short duration.

Medication

Schizophrenia can be treated through antipsychotic medications which are taken on a daily basis. The medication can be in the form of pills or injections which are done on a monthly basis, either once or twice. Since most of the antipsychotic drugs have various side effects, the patients and doctors need to find the best medicine for the patient to limit the adverse consequences. The neuroleptic drugs or tranquillisers help in reducing the symptoms which are positive and contributes to avert relapse. The selection of the type of medicine to use depends on the risks, price, and advantages. Antipsychotic drugs can be either typical or atypical. Antipsychotic drugs have various side effects which include weight gain and diabetes among others. The most commonly prescribed drugs are the olanzapine, risperidone, and quetiapine. When a patient is not responsive to two antipsychotic medications, clozapine can be given as an alternative (Pollak et al., 2004).

Psychosocial Treatment

This kind of treatment is beneficial when the doctor and the patient decide on the kind of treatment which is suitable for the patient. Some of the psychosocial treatments include therapy which involves the family and cognitive behavioural therapy. The treatment may also include giving the patients training on their skills and managing their weight. Interventions which are psychosocial are also used for patients who abuse drugs; the psychosocial treatment is effective for patients with schizophrenia even without the use of medicine (Morrison et al., 2014). The cognitive behavioural therapy targets particular symptoms and helps the patient on issues that involve their esteem and their social function. This treatment enables the patients to know how to manage their feelings. Another kind of therapy is the cognitive remediation therapy which aims at providing remedy to the deficits which are neurocognitive and are usually seen in patients having schizophrenia.

Family therapy focuses on the entire family of the individuals who has been diagnosed with schizophrenia. Families of people living with schizophrenia can benefit from this therapy in cases where the treatment is for an extended period. The family therapy helps in lessening the hurdles which come as a result of the schizophrenia's symptoms. Psychoeducation is done to educate the patient on the illness and to identify the early symptoms and the treatment methods available. The family can be involved in psychoeducation to manage the patient effectively. In instances where other kinds of treatments fail, electroconvulsive therapy can be used.

Early Intervention Teams

People or patients who may be having schizophrenia for the first time can get help from the response team. The team consists mental health professionals who include psychologists, psychiatrists, nurses trained in mental health support, and social workers.

Prevention Strategies for Schizophrenia

Early intervention and treatment can help in the prevention of schizophrenia; the prevention strategies can either be primary, secondary, or tertiary. The primary strategy aims at the reduction of the occurrence rate of the illness; the method used here is studying how childbirth and the development of the foetus influence the occurrence of schizophrenia. The second primary preventive technique is understanding how genes affect incidences of occurrence of schizophrenia, especially for identical twins that bear the same kind of genes. Children whose attention is impaired have been used to predict whether they will develop schizophrenia later in life or not.

The secondary prevention strategy is done by studying the period between the beginning of the symptoms and the time that the schizophrenia disorder is fully recognised. This period is known as the prodromal period. The symptoms in this stage may not necessarily be for schizophrenia; they can be an indication of other mental illnesses and disorders. At the prodromal stage, the patient is examined to establish if they are at a risk of developing schizophrenia later in their lives. If the tests indicate that the patient is in danger of developing schizophrenia later, the treatment procedure commences.

The tertiary preventive strategies include treating individuals who are experiencing their first psychotic episode. The kind of therapy given is aggressive to prevent the illness from progressing further. The patients during the first psychotic episode may require little medication and tend to have a higher rate of response to treatment.

Personality Disorders

According to the American Psychiatric Association (2000), personality compositions are shaped by the perception of the world of an individual. People suffering from personality disorders are gifted with special glasses which are called prisma. Those glasses are invisible for lay people, but they change the world of an individual affected by the disorder. Based on *DSM-5*, there are ten common personality disorders.

Obsessive-Compulsive Personality Disorder

This disorder is characterised by a need for perfection and an extreme stubbornness. In general, people affected by this disorder have lost control over their lives; therefore, in order to gain the loss, they can easily break the privacy of others and try to control them, using their own moral and ethical standards which are usually not accepted by the society.

Dependent Personality Disorder

This disorder causes the individual to have an uncontrolled need to depend on others because of lack of self-confidence. In addition, such need can cause a fear of separation as well as uncertainty and difficulty making any decision without help or approval. In some cases, an individual is willing to do unpleasant things just to gain security and support.

Avoidant Personality Disorder

People affected by this disorder are perceiving the world as a place where everybody is criticising them. As a consequence of that, they are experiencing strong fear of rejection, criticism, displeasure, and embarrassment. These difficulties can prevent them to engage in new relationships or projects.

Narcissistic Personality Disorder

A 'special person' or person suffering from narcissistic personality disorder lives in their own talented world built on their unique power, beauty, self-importance, and grandiosity. The need for 'high status' makes them arrogant, unempathetic, and advantageous of others in order to succeed. The most dangerous narcissists are malignant narcissists because they are enjoying hurting others.

Histrionic Personality Disorder

Attention-seeking patterns make individuals with this disorder draw attention to themselves all the time. Their speech is characterised by lacking details with a lot of strong opinions without abilities to present any evidence for it. They must be in the centre of attention; otherwise, they may do something dramatic to draw the attention. They constantly look for compliments. Because of difficulties to control their emotions, especially jealousy, they may embarrass their loved ones in public by using inappropriate words.

Borderline Personality Disorder

Characterised by instability, anger, anxiety, panic, depressive moods, distorted self-image, and impulsivity, people who suffer from this disorder are very sensitive to their environment. In order to deal with these difficulties, they often engage in risky behaviour, such as gambling or unsafe sex. Shame and guilt may result because of the impulsive behaviour.

Antisocial Personality Disorder

Difficulty to follow the norms and rules, disrespect for the law, inability to plan, execute, and evaluate as well as irrationality and aggressiveness can cause people harm our society.

Schizotypal Personality Disorder

This disorder makes people believe in magic or superstitiousness. They have difficulty creating close relationships because of their paranoia and delusions caused by distorted perception and cognition.

Schizoid Personality Disorder

People affected by this disorder are very detached to society. They do not enjoy being next to their loved ones. The lack of emotions and enjoyment in simple things makes these people very lonely, and they usually live by themselves.

Paranoid Personality Disorder

Often people suffering from this disorder believe that others will harm them. They have difficulty keeping relationships because of their trust issues and doubts.

Treatment of Personality Disorders

In general, a combination of SSRIs and dialectical behavioural therapy (DBT) is the best treatment option for the moment in treating personality disorders. The main issue in treating the disorders is to make clients aware of their actions. Poor awareness or poor insight is the biggest barrier to make changes in the client's perception of the words.

Impulse Control Disorders

These disorders can be defined as disorders caused by lack of impulse control. Fear of engaging in some behaviours can actually disappear during such actions. The most common impulse control disorders are pyromania, kleptomania, pathological gambling, and uncontrolled shopping (Tolin, 2007).

Therapy

Commonly, SSRIs and cognitive behavioural therapy (CBT) are the most successful therapies used in treating impulse control disorder.

CHAPTER 2

Stigma And Mental Illness

Stigma can be defined as a stereotype which is negative; it is also the demeaning attitude which a society or community can have towards people who seem different based on their religion, race, or medical condition. Stigma occurs when the public or a person holds beliefs which are contrary towards a particular situation or circumstance. The words *stigma* and *discrimination* are usually used together though they mean different things. Stigmatisation happens when a person is seen to be different from other people, while bias or discrimination is where an individual is given a different treatment from other people in the society. Also, discrimination is where an individual receives treatment which is unjust because of their identity. The bias can occur because of the person's gender, age, economic or marital status, race among others. Stigmatisation, on the other hand, happens when a person is considered as being contaminated or marred. Though different, stigma and discrimination go together especially to those who are affected by mental illness.

The stigma against people who are affected by mental illness began in the early twentieth century. Most of these people were put in asylums, often without their consent. Patients were placed in rooms which were overcrowded; therapies included lobotomies and isolation. Despite the progress in medicine on mental health, the stigma against these people continues. There are various examples which show stigma against those who are affected by mental illness, which include looking at those affected by mental illness as being unstable. Another example of stigma against those who are affected by mental illness is where a person affected by schizophrenia is regarded as dangerous. Stigma also views people in psychiatric hospitals as insane, and people affected by bipolar disorder are looked at as hard or difficult to understand.

There are various models which explain stigma. One of them is the social cognitive model which describes the relationship that exists among the signals or cues, the attitudes, and the resultant stigma. The stigma cues can involve the person affected by mental illness starting to talk to themselves; this results in negative stereotypes or views, where the society tends to avoid the affected individual. The attitude leads to stigma, and at times, the community may decide not to reside in the same locality with this individual.

The Social Cognitive Model

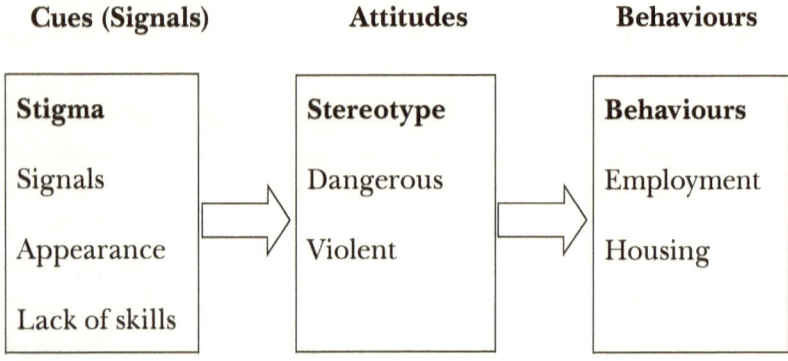

Cues (Signals)	Attitudes	Behaviours
Stigma Signals Appearance Lack of skills	**Stereotype** Dangerous Violent	**Behaviours** Employment Housing

Stigma considers a person as being of less value in comparison to the other members of the society. Stigma is usually a sign or mark of dishonour or shame, while discrimination is treating a person as being different. Stigma for the people affected by mental illness has its origin in history, where in the Middle Ages, mental illness was seen to be a result of a demonic possession. Because of this, those affected were kept in isolation to exorcise the demons. The first mental hospitals were places where there was torture for those affected by mental illness. An example is in Bedlam, which was an asylum in London. The people affected by mental illness were exhibited in public for a small amount of money from the viewers, while others went to the streets to beg. These patients were also tortured in the early mental hospitals and subjected to inhumane acts. For example, in the first hospitals, patients with depression underwent electroshock therapy and lobotomy as a form of treatment.

On mental illness, stigma happens when the judgements, opinions, and stereotypes are cynical about people with mental illness and disorders of any kind. The individuals affected by mental illness are referred to as mad, crazy, lunatics. All these names are stigmatising these people. Those affected are given different treatment which is in contrast to the treatment which other members of the community receive. By treating those who have mental illness in such a manner, it worsens the challenges which they face in connection with the illness, and their recovery process becomes more laborious.

There are various views which the society holds towards different types of mental illness. Some of the views include people with schizophrenia cannot be predicted and are dangerous (Crisp et al., 2000). In addition, individuals who have drug and alcohol addictions or dependence are seen as dangerous and to blame for their habits (Crisp et al., 2005). Some culture also holds the belief that mental illness makes a person less intelligent and unable to make any decisions (Angermeyer & Matschinger, 2005). People who have depression are seen as being lazy and difficult to communicate with (Thornicroft, 2006). Young people between the ages of sixteen to nineteen years seem to have more negative attitudes towards those affected by mental illness in comparison to any other group of people (Crisp et al., 2005).

Stigma brings with it a double challenge to those with mental illness. The individual struggles with the illness and the negative attitude which the society has towards them because of the illness. Because of this challenge, these people rarely get chances of having a life of quality. Their chances of living in safe neighbourhoods and houses and getting good jobs and healthcare are minimal. People with mental illnesses face stigma from their friends, family, co-workers, and employers. Because of stigmatisation, some of the people with mental illness and disorders may be reluctant to look for help in health facilities to hide their condition.

There are various components of stigma. The first is that the sick person is seen to be weak and not ill. For example, a person with depression, since they have periods when they cannot wake from bed, are taken to be weak and not sick. The second element or component of stigma is when the person is seen to be dangerous. This mostly applies to patients having schizophrenia; because of their behaviours, the society views them as being dangerous. The third component which constitutes stigma is when there is the belief that the person can control their actions and thoughts. An example is when a person with bipolar disorder experiences manic episodes; rather than getting mental healthcare, there is an expectation that they learn on how to control themselves.

Another component of stigma is that the sick person tends to keep to themselves because of shame and guilt regarding their condition. The other element that comprises stigma is that the ill person may be unwilling to reveal their status because of the fear of stigma and discrimination. Stigma is also associated with the sick person or their caregivers becoming socially distant. Those affected by mental illness are seen as people who should be feared and excluded from the society. Also, they are regarded as irresponsible, so decisions should be made for them regarding their lives. The society also believes that people with mental disorders need to be taken care of as small children.

The Causes of Stigma towards Mental Illness

Some of the causes or reasons for stigma in relation to mental illness include the idea that the individuals affected by mental illness are dangerous and erratic. Also, religion has blamed sickness on sin; thus, the ill person or their family may be viewed as sinners because of their condition. Religion also associates mental illness to evil spirits and demons. This causes stigma to those with the illness. The community also views the person with a mental disorder as lacking in various ways. Some of the ways which the society sees the person as lacking is them having no moral power and being unable to give back to the community. This makes the society to stigmatise against the person affected by mental illness.

The individual affected by mental illness may behave differently from the other people. An example is when people having schizophrenia may become aggressive. This makes people in the society afraid of them. This, in turn, increases the level of stigma that the person encounters. This is exceptionally high in India since most of the people in the society do not know much mental illness, especially schizophrenia (Thera et al., 2000). Another cause of stigma towards the person affected by mental illness is culture. There are myths in various communities about mental illness. An example is when people with schizophrenia are seen as being violent or having a dual personality.

Moreover, the history associated with the treatment of mental illness initially put fear in the society and brought an increase in stigmatisation to the people affected by mental illness. During the early days when these people went to the mental hospitals, the society did not expect them to return. In some cultures, the subject of mental illness is a taboo, and since there is no one to bring clarity concerning mental illness, the stigma continues and remains within that community. Another cause of stigma against those who are affected by mental illness is that, in the society, wealth makes one be regarded as being successful. Those in the community with no material wealth are seen as unsuccessful, which includes those affected by mental illness, thus discriminating against them.

Some of the medications which these individuals use have adverse effects on their physical bodies and behaviours. Some of the adverse effects of the medicines can include having their eyes twitch and shuffling while walking. These and other physical signs can make people shun the sick individual. Since mental illness and health is a subject rarely taught in schools, consecutive generations grow up with wrong images regarding mental illness. When these people come across a person affected by mental illness, the chances of stigmatising them is high since they do not have information about mental illness.

In some communities, mental illness is related to judgement; this means that the sick person is the one at fault. This also brings stigma to the people affected by mental illness since they are seen as having caused their illness. The ill individual may isolate themself from the rest of the society because of shame. People may misunderstand this and spread rumours, which can further increase the stigma that the person faces. Children who may not understand the behaviour of a person affected by mental illness may make them an object of their fun, not realising the impact that it has on the individual.

As the treatments for the physical and mental illness are divided, this makes mental illnesses and disorders seem different to other kinds of illnesses. Some people experience self-worth by bringing others down or discriminating against them. People who are affected by mental sickness become the target of these people, further increasing stigma against these people. Some mental illness can cause a person to behave bizarrely. Those around them may not understand the behaviour, and they may stigmatise the sick person. Some communities believe that mental illness originated from the supernatural world (Gureje & Alem, 2000).

A person affected by mental illness may not feel comfortable or at ease talking about their condition. This makes the people around the ill individual sometimes to interpret what the ill person is experiencing inaccurately, thus causing stigma. Ignorance causes stigmatisation to those who are affected by mental illnesses; this brings fear when dealing with the person. Media is a primary cause of stigma for people affected by mental illness; there are various films and horror movies which depict mental illness negatively. As a result, the society tends to view a person affected by mental illness as being different, further increasing the stigma towards mental illness.

The Impact of Stigma Towards People Affected by Mental Illness

Stigma is still evidenced in the society today; it can affect the people affected by mental illness in various ways (Corrigan, 2004). One of the ways is where the self-esteem of the sick person is negatively affected by not being given the opportunities which are available socially. In most instances, people may not want to associate themselves with a person affected by mental illness. An example is when a sick person is not given the opportunity to take care of their children or even get into any meaningful relationship (Corrigan et al., 2001). Another way in which stigma impacts a person affected by mental illness is self-rejection as a result of the rejection that they receive from the society (Livingstone & Boyd, 2010).

Because of stigma, a sick person may become withdrawn and lack in confidence because of the continuous ridicule by the society.

Stigma also has led to physical abuse to the people affected by mental illness from neighbours and strangers. At times, there is the destruction of their property, and some shops or recreational facilities tend to bar those who are affected by mental illness.

Some people affected by mental illness are addressed as children or lacking in understanding (Lyons et al., 2009). This contributes to the individual having feelings of fear, anger, anxiety, isolation among others. At times, the individual may visit a health professional, and on expressing the symptoms they could be experiencing, they are dismissed by the health personnel (Lyons et al., 2009). The impact of this is that the person may be unwilling or reluctant to visit a health professional in future. This may put their health at risk since they are prone to other health problems, such as diabetes, obesity, and respiratory illness (Social Exclusion Unit, 2004).

Mental illness can cause relationships with one's family, partners, and friends to break down. There are also instances of bullying of the children of the individuals affected by mental illness because of their parents' illness (SEU, 2004). Stigma can hinder a person from seeking early treatment for symptoms related to mental illness. The result is that the individual may look for cure when the mental illness is more severe and harder to treat. The sick person may feel helpless and hopeless. The affected person tends to lose friends once they have been diagnosed with mental illness; very few people want their association (Gureje et al., 2005). Even after treatment, the society may not accept entirely the person who had mental illness previously. The family and caregivers may abandon the sick individual in the hospital, not wanting to have any association with them.

The individual affected by mental illness can start believing what those around say concerning them. Their thought pattern can become harmful and can quickly lead to death through suicide. To avoid people labelling them as being affected by mental illness, the person may hide their condition and refuse to look for healthcare. The result is that the state of the person may become worse, and the recovery becomes difficult.

Impact of Stigma in the Workplace

Stigma causes those with mental illness to lack employment opportunities. They may apply for jobs which they have the right qualifications for, but because of the illness, they may not get the job (Alexander & Link, 2000). For the individuals who are already employed and are affected by mental sickness, their colleagues at work may treat them differently; this leads to many of them hiding their condition from their colleagues (Bos et al., 2009). In the workplace, co-workers of the sick person may make fun of them at times because of the adverse effect of the medication. An example is some medication used by an individual with schizophrenia can result in them having tremors which are physically visible, leading to ridicule in the workplace.

Some organisations may not employ an individual who is affected by mental illness since they are regarded as being unable to perform their duties. Other employers feel they would experience loss of customers on hiring a person affected by mental illness. Some mental illness continuously recurs. This may make an employer unwilling to engage a person affected by mental illness (Stier & Hinshaw, 2007). In some organisations, an individual affected by mental illness can be laid off from work because of taking time off to attend therapy. An individual who has depression may be viewed as being lazy by both the employer and co-workers. Because of fear of discrimination and stigma, the sick person may not reveal their condition upon employment.

Impact of Stigma on Accessing Health for Those Affected by Mental Illness

Some health professional stigmatises against patients with mental illness. When these patients visit the hospitals, a health professional, upon realising that the patients have mental illness, may not pay attention to their other concerns about physical symptoms which they may be experiencing. An example is where a patient who has an anxiety disorder may report to a general health practitioner about some physical pain they may be experiencing. The health practitioner, knowing the history of the patient, may conclude that this is a panic attack. The patient may suffer embarrassment and shame and refuse in future to seek any medical care; this can result in death through suicide or health-related issues. General practitioners may have a negative attitude towards those who are affected by mental illness in comparison to psychologists and psychiatrists.

Impact of Stigma on the Caregivers

Stigma does not affect the sick individual only, but their caregivers, the family, and the relatives too as they receive exclusion from the society (Corrigan et al., 2006). In some instances, the caregivers get embarrassed publicly. Also, some communities can become hostile towards the caregivers. Stigma and discrimination can cause the sick person with their families to stay in secrecy without interacting with other people. Because of stigma, caregivers may rarely share with other people the burden or issues that they could be facing in taking care of a person affected by mental illness. Stigma increases the responsibility of taking care of the individual since the family, in most cases, does not receive support from the society.

At times, caregivers may need leave from work to take care of the sick person. The employer may want to know the reason for their absence, and on explaining, the caregiver may start to experience stigma and discrimination in the workplace. Parents who are primary caregivers for their children tend to be blamed for having a child who is affected by mental illness; there is criticism concerning their parenting skills. In some communities, a parent is usually advised against taking care of their ill child. Some societies also avoid involving caregivers in social functions; moreover, families of the sick person are rarely visited.

Caregivers usually receive negative comments about the care which they are giving. At times, the society will criticise caregivers when they defend the ill individual. The relatives of people who are affected by mental illness are usually blamed for the illness, causing them to encounter shame. The result is that these caregivers will tend to avoid friends and neighbours.

Models of Mental Illness Stigma

There are various models which can help in explaining how personal and societal traits influence the views, attitudes, behaviours, and beliefs held towards people affected by mental illnesses. They include the following:

Social Psychological Model

This model holds the assumption that values, attitudes, and beliefs are displayed during interpersonal or social communication and interactions (Goffman, 1969). The knowledge or understanding of mental illness obtained early in life is applied by the individual on themselves or others later in their life. An individual who expects rejection and discrimination may avoid interacting with others, and this tends to impact adversely on the person's self-esteem (Rosenfield, 1997).

Attribution Model

This model holds the assumption that a person who is affected by mental illness, is responsible for their illness, thus stigmatising against them. Since the person is viewed as having control of their condition, they tend to be blamed if they are unable to control their symptoms (Corrigan, 2000). An example is in the Asian culture where being unable to control one's emotions and feelings is seen as a sign of weakness. Since in most mental illnesses, the affected person cannot control the symptoms, then according to the attribution model, they are weak, which worsens the stigma which they experience (Lin & Cheung, 1999).

Image of the Attribution Model

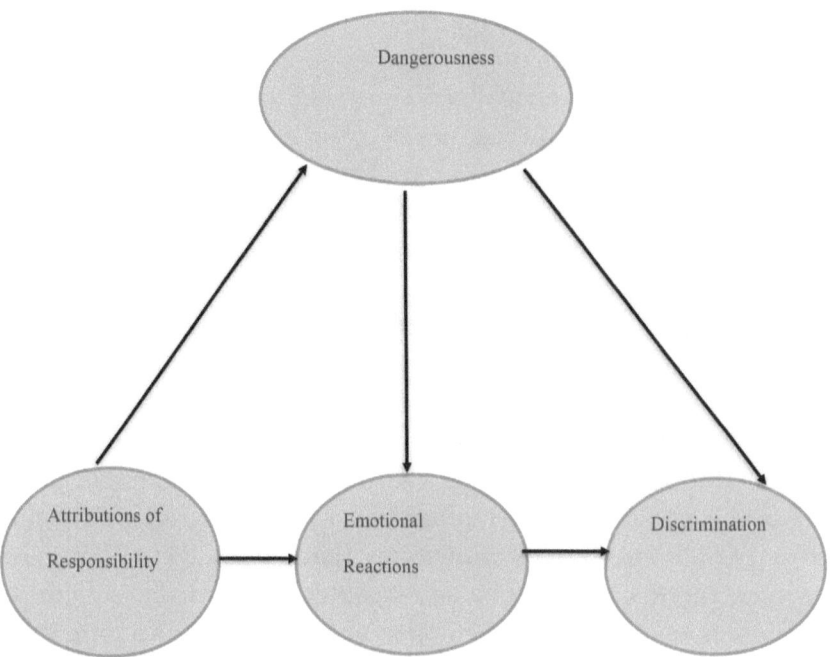

The Types of Stigma

There are two classifications of stigma associated with mental illness, namely, social stigma and self- or perceived stigma.

Social/Public Stigma and Mental Illness

Social or public stigma refers to the beliefs and attitudes which the public or the general population has towards people affected by mental illness or their caregivers, which include their families. This stigma comprises stereotypes, discrimination, and prejudice, where those affected by mental illness get discriminated by the society because of the stereotype held by the society towards mental illness. In social stigma, an individual suffers discrimination, where friends and family may avoid them. It becomes difficult for the affected person to get housing, employment, or even access to healthcare.

These people also, because of stigma, cannot have a meaningful relationship. They may have a desire to marry, but because of discrimination and stigma, they cannot marry. In China, for example, those affected by mental illness, together with their immediate family members, are not allowed to marry since the Chinese society attribute mental illness to the misconduct of one's ancestors. Religion also discriminates against those who are affected by mental illness by denying the existence of mental sickness or indicating that the cause of the illness is supernatural. In cases of crime, the police tend not to believe the person's report or account.

Public stigma has various forms of expressions which include refusing to help a person affected by mental illness and avoiding the person. Forcing a person to do things unwillingly is another way of publicly stigmatising the person. Putting the people affected by mental illness in institutions where they are segregated is also a way of the public stigmatising against them. Public stigma begins when people see signals indicating that an individual may be having a mental illness. The signs could be physically noticeable on the person's behaviour or appearance. When indications show that a person is affected by mental illness, there is the activation of stereotype (Corrigan, 2004). An example of a stereotype is that all those affected by mental illness are aggressive and violent. What follows the stereotype is discrimination. In comparison to other physical ailments, people with mental illness experience more stigma and discrimination.

Public Stigma Model

Cue ⟶ Cognition ⟶ Behaviour

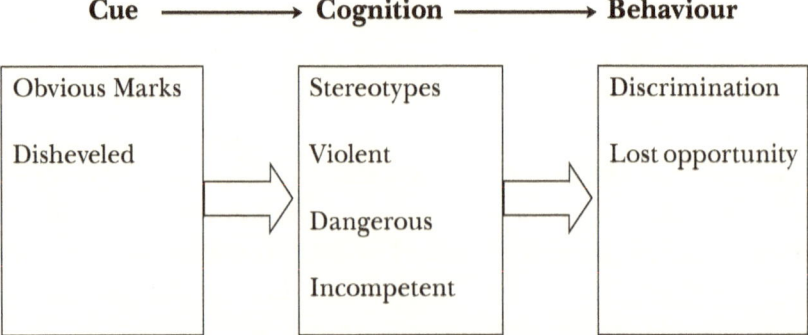

Obvious Marks	Stereotypes	Discrimination
Disheveled	Violent	Lost opportunity
	Dangerous	
	Incompetent	

How Public Stigma Impacts on the People Affected by Mental Illness

Public stigma has many effects on an individual affected by mental illness. Some of the impacts include discrimination. In accordance to Overton and Medina (2008), landlords rarely rent out their houses to a person who is affected by mental illness. It is also highly unlikely for employers to hire a person affected by mental illness. At times, when the person is employed, they may tend to be paid less in comparison to other people whom they work together with.

A person affected by mental illness also receives cues or attitudes which are both hostile and negative from the public or the society where they live. The result is that the ill individual may decide to discontinue the treatment to avoid being treated differently (Gonzales et al., 2015). The public views the people affected by mental illness as being less intelligent or even dangerous. The family or caregivers of the sick individual can advise them not to reveal their condition to anyone; this can bar them from receiving proper treatment (Gonzales et al., 2015). The public or society also tends to avoid an individual affected by mental illness. Public stigma can aggravate the signs of psychopathology.

A person affected by mental illness can be discriminated against on an individual or institutional level which is referred to as a structural stigma. An example is where one-third of the states in the United States of America do not allow a person with mental sickness to hold an elective post. In these states, a person cannot vote or take part in juries. According to Corrigan, Markowitz, and Watson (2004), some of these states deny parents who are affected by mental illness custody of their children. These hindrances are a result of the person being classified as being affected by mental illness and not by them being incompetent in raising their children or holding elective posts.

Public stigma can cause a person affected by mental illness not to seek treatment to avoid their friends or colleagues at work from knowing their condition (Corrigan, 2004). The fear is because when their status becomes public, their friends, colleagues, and neighbours can have a negative opinion of them. Because of delay in seeking treatment because of fear of public stigmatisation, when the person finally looks for treatment, it may be too late, or the recovery process may take an extended period. Public stigma can also lead to suicide since the person is unable to handle the criticism. All mental illnesses are linked to public stigma, but there are certain types of mental illnesses which experience more stigmas from both the health professionals and the society. Some of these illnesses include schizophrenia, bipolar disorders, borderline personality disorders among others. A health professional may tend to assume during therapy that a person with borderline personality disorder is exaggerating their reaction (Aviram, Brodsky, & Stanley, 2006).

Professionals in mental health can also stigmatise patients affected by mental illness. Also, some of the beliefs that mental health professionals hold concerning these patients are erroneous. An example is that these people are destined to fail in life (Corrigan, 2002). Some health professionals also hold the view that people with schizophrenia are different from other people. At times, some health professionals do not give hope of recovery to the patients affected by mental illness.

Ways of Reducing Public Stigma

There are various ways of fighting public stigma towards the person. They include education, protest, and social contact. These are useful tools in the fight against public stigma (Michaels et al., 2013).

Advocacy and Protest

Advocacy and protest refer to formally objecting the negative depiction towards those who are affected by mental illness. The people who have been stigmatised are the first to begin the protest together with those advocating for them. The demonstrations may involve boycotting specific products, conducting public demonstrations, and writing letters to those promoting stigma. The groups which are the primary targets for the protests and advocacy are political leaders, community leaders, and journalists. The protest targets the media, advertisements, and public statements which stigmatise those who are affected by mental illness. The Internet is a useful tool in advocating changes regarding mental illness. Mental health professionally uses the online platform as an advocacy tool in educating the public on mental illness to reduce the stigma associated with the illness (Peek et al., 2015).

The campaign aims at encouraging people with mental illness, together with their families, to seek health services. The campaigns can be done at the school level where the schools are encouraged to introduce programmes which will educate the students on mental health issues. The knowledge which the student gets can help in changing their attitudes, behaviour, and knowledge regarding mental illness. Though protest reduces views which are contrary, it does not promote attitudes which are positive; it only suppresses the negative thoughts the public has towards the people affected by mental illness.

Face-to-Face Contact

The second strategy which can help reduce public stigma against those who are affected by mental illness is interacting directly with the ill person and their families or caregivers. This intervention whose basis is face-to-face contact helps reduce public stigma since the ill individual gets the feeling that they are seen to be in equal status with the other members of the society. The direct contact helps in changing the behaviour which the public has towards those who are affected by mental illness (Overton & Medina, 2008).

At times, videos and films showing the experiences of those affected by mental illness and their caregivers and families can be used as a way of making direct contact. By doing this, the public will not distance themselves from those who are affected by mental illness (Hackler, Cornish, & Vogel, 2016). This strategy or tool is useful but time-consuming and costly regarding the cost to be incurred in establishing the direct contact with the patient. The success of this approach relies on the circumstances surrounding the direct contact and the type of contact.

The more the public interacts with those who are affected by mental illness, the less likely they are to perceive them as being different. An example is those people who have colleagues at work or friends who are affected by mental illness stigmatise them less in comparison with the people who had no contact with the sick person. For social contact to be sufficient, there should be similarities between the target audience and the person doing the presentation. Establishing contact can be done in learning institutions which include colleges where students affected by mental illness can discuss with other students concerning their experiences.

The introduction of social media helps those patients with mental disorders who may not be able or willing to have face-to-face interactions to discuss their experiences. This is most common among the young people with mental illness who may wish to talk about their challenges with the illness anonymously (Suzuki & Calzo, 2004). Contact and education can be used together in reducing stigma about mental illness.

Utilisation of Peer Services

Peer services groups consist of people who have had an experience with mental illness, working as healthcare providers. They help those who have mental illness to be able to face the challenges which they may be encountering and may include stigma. The peer service also helps in negating the stigma and discrimination which the person can comes across when seeking for treatment. These services help in advancing the rights of the people affected by mental illness. Their rights are promoted by assisting them to get more employment opportunities and treatment.

Education

Education is another tool that can help reduce public stigma among the people affected by mental illness. The reason stems from the fact that stigma is usually a result of lack of knowledge by the public regarding mental illnesses. Education will aim at informing both the public and health professionals and removing incorrect stereotypes about mental illness. When people have sufficient knowledge on the causes and treatment for mental illness, it can lower the negative attitudes and rejections which those who are affected by mental illness encounter (Mannarin & Bofo, 2014). This approach has some limitations which include only those who accept and agree with the information given regarding mental illness will change their views.

An example of an educational approach is when there is the countering of the idea that those with mental illness are murderers. This can be done by showing that rates of homicide are similar between those affected by mental illness and the public in general (Corrigan et al., 2012). The educational strategies can either be done in the local or national level.

Campaigns on Mental Health Literacy

In reducing public stigma, campaigns where the public are educated on mental health are a necessary tool. This tool can be used in schools where programmes on mental health are taught and incorporated into the curriculum (Wei et al., 2013). These programmes help in improving the attitudes, knowledge, and behaviour that the students will have towards those who are affected by mental illness in the school. The literacy programmes in school help in reducing stigma among the schoolgoing children. The campaign's focus is on encouraging both the person affected by mental illness and their family to look for the health services.

Self-stigma and Mental Illness

The second type of stigma on mental illness is self-stigma, which happens when the person who is affected by mental illness agrees or accepts the attitudes from the public which are harmful and uses them against themself. Self-stigma, which is also known as the perceived stigma, occurs when the sick person tends to internalise the stigma from the public. The feeling that the person is not living according to the socially accepted standard may cause them to experience self-stigma (Overton & Medina, 2008). Since the person agrees with what the society says about mental illness, the individual develops a negative stereotype.

Some of the stereotypes of self-stigma include the person beginning to see themself as being dangerous or incompetent. The person then develops negative emotions, discriminating themself from others; a low self-esteem comes as a result. Self-stigma reduces the feelings of self-worth of an individual who is affected by mental illness. The quality of a person's life decreases because of the sense of worthlessness.

Self-stigma makes the individual have no interest in pursuing their life's goals or achieving anything in life. The individual may remain unemployed since they think there is no need of looking for employment as they tend to feel worthless. The person may also believe that no employer would be willing to hire them. The individual may also not see the need to either have their own home or have any relationship. The cause of this is that the person at this stage is suffering from the effect referred to as Why Try.

Self-stigma Progressive Model

Self-stigma can be shown in a progressive stage model which has four stages or steps. The first step is awareness of the stereotype where the person becomes conscious that the society devalues or looks down on those who are affected by mental illness. The second stage of the progressive model is where the individual agrees with the stereotype that the public has towards mental illness. The third step is where there is self-occurrence, and the individual starts to believe that the stereotype or the negative attitude towards mental illness applies to them personally. The fourth stage of the progressive model of self-stigma is where the self-esteem of a person affected by mental illness starts to diminish as a result of accepting the stereotype and applies it to themself personally.

Awareness:
The public believes
people with mental
illness are weak.

Agreement:
That's right. People
with mental illness
are weak.

Apply:
I am mentally ill so I
must be weak.

Harm:
Because I am weak, I
am not worthy or
able.

Why try...
To pursue a job; I am not worthy.
To live on my own; I am not able.

Self-stigma has various effects on the person affected by mental illness; one of the effects is that the self-esteem of the person diminishes (Watson et al., 2007). The individual may experience self-doubt concerning the ability to function normally. Self-stigma can cause depression and reduces the rate of progress during therapy. Self-stigma can also cause the person not to have the desire to seek for employment since they feel no employer would be willing to hire them.

Self-stigma can become a hindrance in seeking for treatment because of the stereotype surrounding mental illness (Matschinger & Angermeyer, 2009). The person may tend to avoid seeking treatment or may drop out of therapy since they do not want to suffer any stigma by being referred to as one affected by mental illness.

Ways of Reducing Self-stigma

The first step in challenging self-stigma is for the individual affected by mental illness to reveal their condition to other people. The person should avoid hiding in shame. By exposing and disclosing their illness, they can counter shame. By disclosing their condition, the person may find friends and families who are willing to give them support. These individuals may begin to gain control and power over their lives. Though disclosure has a positive impact, there are also adverse effects that come out of it. Some of the adverse outcomes include experiencing discrimination from their families and friends. An example is in India; if there is a documentation to the effect that an individual has a mental illness, then that becomes a ground for divorce.

To avoid adverse effects which arise from disclosure, a sick person can choose to disclose their condition selectively. This kind of disclosure is where the information concerning the mental illness is given to a specific group of people only. The groups of people who are privy to the information on mental illness may include support group and close family members among others.

The second approach in reducing self-stigma is an intervention on ending self-stigma. This strategy or approach uses groups in lowering self-stigma. The group organises meetings where education is provided about mental health. The group also discusses ways of strengthening social and family relationships. The members of the group learn cognitive behavioural approaches through cognitive therapy. An example of cognitive therapy is where a sick individual is taught on how to challenge statements which they make and which are irrational. Some of the comments or statements include the person stating that they have depression because they are stupid. During therapy, the person is taught how to challenge this.

An example is a programme which was developed in the United States; the programme's name is National Alliance on Mental illness. The programme has helped in the reduction of attitudes which are cynical about people with mental illness. This, in turn, has reduced self-stigma among individuals who are affected by mental illness.

Mental Illness and the Media

For most people, media is the primary source of information which they have concerning many issues of life, including mental illnesses and disorders (Wahl, 2004). The media consists of the mass media, that is, the newspapers, movies, television shows, and other publications (Giddens, 2006). There is also the social media, which includes the Facebook, Twitter, WhatsApp, and other forms of social media. There are stereotypes and negative information given in media regarding mental illness. Some of the stereotypes include labelling people who commit crimes which are violent 'schizophrenics' and 'mentally ill' by the media. Crimes can be committed by people who are not affected by mental illness. This contradicts what the media portrays in connection with those who are affected by mental illness.

When the media gives erroneous and misleading information, the public will tend to believe the information; this will have a negative impact on those who are affected by mental illness. The information which the media portrays concerning mental illness is mostly negative, erroneous, or stereotypical. The myths which the media uses to describe mental illness influence the public's perception of mental illness. An example is when people watch television where people with schizophrenia are depicted negatively. The person watching may not want any association with the person who has schizophrenia (Angermeyer et al., 2005). The stigma against those who are mentally sick increases because of the myths portrayed by the media. The media often portrays those who are affected by mental illness as being responsible for their condition.

Misrepresentation of Mental Illness by Newspapers and Magazines

Most newspapers portray all mental illnesses as being the same; most newspaper reports relate mental illness to violence, crime, and danger. Also, people affected by mental illness are described as people deserving pity (Goulden et al., 2011). Newspapers also differentiate people who have mental illness from those who are mentally healthy (Olstead, 2002). Most articles which report on schizophrenia depict the people with the illness as being violent (Goulden, 2011). Anorexia tends to be seen as a condition of white females who are young (Saguy & Gruys, 2010).

Depression in some magazines, such as the *Australian Women's Weekly* magazine in 2005, was portrayed as a personal problem and that the affected person was in a position to manage it (Gattuso et al., 2005). This portrayal by the media is different with the national action plan for depression in Australia, which states that depression requires treatment from mental health professionals.

Misrepresentation of Mental Illness by Television

Television has a detrimental influence on attitudes and beliefs regarding mental illness (Diefenbach & West, 2007). According to Stuart (2006), children start watching TV at an early age where images of various issues, including mental illness, are imprinted in their minds. The movies where there are characters who are affected by mental illness train children on how to respond to people who are affected when they meet with them.

Television influences the basis of society's perceptions of those people who are affected by mental illness. Television shows people who are affected by mental illness as being dangerous and violent. Since the society rarely interacts with those who have a mental illness, the only source of information they have regarding mental illness is the media and, more particularly, the television (Stout et al., 2004). Television news uses mental illness in their headlines to get the attention of the public; this strengthens the stigma towards those with mental illness. How the society responds to those with mental illness begins by watching characters in television shows who have mental illness. The characters display those who have mental disorders as people living in isolation, having no families or jobs. These attitudes are later taken into real life and determine how the public views and treats the people with mental disorders.

Television series and films also portray mental health practitioners as being inhuman and evil. They are described as being more mentally affected in comparison to their patients. The society uses television as the primary source of their information regarding mental illness. This has an impact on the public, that is, what is seen on the screen is regarded as reality (Stout et al., 2004). The more the public watches programmes on television which portrays those affected by mental illness negatively, the more the public becomes intolerant of these people. Television mostly describes the person affected by mental illness using their illness as their identity. Some television shows involving crime attribute crime to mental illness.

Television also misrepresents some of the treatment methods of mental illness. An example is an electroconvulsive treatment which is depicted as being a means of punishing uncontrollable patients (McFarquhar & Thomson, 2008). By misrepresenting the procedure, both the public and the one affected by the mental illness become wary of using this procedure in their treatment. Television dramas on crimes tend to relate male characters who are affected by mental illness as being more violent in comparison to their female counterparts.

Media Stereotypes about Mental Illness

Some of the stereotypes which the media depicts on mental illness include people who are affected by mental illness are violent, dangerous, incompetent, and have a low level of intelligence. The media has played a significant role in stigmatising the people affected by mental illness. A few examples of the incorrect and false stereotypes which the media portrays concerning those who are affected by mental illness are the following:

People Who Are Affected by Mental Illness Are Violent

Some of the news on the televisions and newspapers depict the person affected by mental illness as one who hurts or murders innocent people. Newspapers influence the public in reporting of violence which is connected to those who are affected by mental illness. An example is when a violent crime occurs, and there is news coverage, the media will—in most cases—portray the perpetrator as being affected by mental illness. By doing this, the media downplays the seriousness of the crime by indicating that an individual affected by mental illness committed the crime. The second thing is by downplaying the seriousness of the crime. The message sent across to the public is that there is nothing good that can be expected from those who are affected by mental illness. In reality, there are many crimes committed by people who are not affected by mental illness (Monahan, 1996).

Media misrepresentation influences the public; an example is a fear that was put to the people after the 11 September 2001, terrorist attack in America. The media presented the planes as a dangerous mode of transport which put the fear of flying among many people. People opted to drive many miles, increasing the likelihood of an accident because of fatigue, and having many vehicles on the road brought an increase to road accidents. Death tolls caused by the terrorist attack was lesser in comparison to the deaths caused by car accidents in the same period. One thousand six hundred more accidents were reported on the roads after 11 September 2001, because of the fear of flying in comparison to the previous year (Gaissmaier, 2012).

This is the same thing media does by portraying those who are affected by mental illness as the ones who commit crimes. The public is misled by this depiction since most crimes are committed by people who are not affected by mental illness. The public starts to view those who are affected by mental illness as people who are violent and not in control of their emotions and behaviours. The picture given by the media of the people affected by mental illness is that they are dangerous, unreasonable, and aggressive. Some movies which have characters acting as being mentally sick people portray the ill person as violent. This is especially connected with patients who have schizophrenia.

Physical Appearance of the Person Affected by Mental Illness Is Different in Comparison to Other People

On television, movies, or video games, the person affected by mental illness is shown as having unkempt hair and wearing clothes which are crumpled. This person is also portrayed as having a wild appearance. All these traits are to serve as signals of an evil or dangerous person. This may not be true since some homeless people may have a dishevelled appearance, and they may not be affected by mental illness. On the other hand, there are people affected by mental illness who are clean and well-groomed. Thus, the media depiction of a person affected by mental illness as being physically unkempt is false and misleading to the public.

People Affected by Mental Illness Are Childish and Senseless (Silly)

Some television shows and movies show the person affected by mental illness as being childish and silly. An example is where a person who has an obsessive-compulsive disorder is portrayed by the media as being immature or funny. The person could be struggling with the illness, but the media depiction will influence the public not to take the individual's condition seriously. The result can be not taking the person for treatment, which can worsen the situation.

All Mental Illnesses Are Similar or Equal in Severity

Another stereotype which the media gives to the public concerning mental illness is that mental illness or disorders are all the same. In some instances, the media can portray the symptoms of patients with schizophrenia as being similar to those with bipolar disorder. The media in some occasions use a single name to describe all mental illnesses.

Mental/Psychiatric Hospitals Are Harmful

Some shows in the television and movies show mental hospitals as lacking in comfort and having mental health professionals who are dominating and controlling. Patients in the psychiatric hospitals are shown as being there but not in their volition. This depiction is different from reality since there has been noticeable improvements in the mental health institutions since the eighteenth century. In the early years, the mental facilities were similar to prisons, but today's psychiatric hospitals cater for the patient's comfort. Also, people go to mental hospitals voluntarily without being forced.

There Is No Hope of Recovery for People Affected by Mental Illness

The media shows people affected by mental illness as having no hope for recovery, and if they seek for treatment, seldom does their condition improve. This message by the media indicates that people affected by mental illness are incapable of living a healthy life. The message is erroneous since these patients recover and live a healthy life.

Adolescents or Teenagers with Mental Illness Are Only Going through a Phase

Some movies show teenagers who abuse drugs and alcohol as a typical adolescent behaviour, with the teenager later outgrowing the behaviour. In reality, substance abuse is a mental disorder where the individual should seek treatment.

People with Similar Diagnosis of Mental Illness Have Similar Experience

The media portrays people having the same kind of diagnosis in regard to mental illness experiencing the same type of symptoms. People affected by mental illness could have a similar diagnosis but experience different symptoms, depending on their personality type and environment among other factors.

People Affected by Mental Illness Portrayed as Being Social Outcasts

In the entertainment industry, those who are affected by mental illness are depicted as outcasts in the society. The media portrays them as people who have no employment, homeless, and no family or friends. According to Olstead (2002), people affected by mental illness are seen as having no social identity. This misrepresentation by the media makes people affected by mental illness to be viewed as less of human beings.

Media Misrepresentation of Mental Health Practitioners

In most cases, the media portrays psychiatrists, psychologists, and other mental health practitioners negatively. In most of the films and movies, mental health professionals and facilities are depicted as being affected by mental illness—neurotic, uncaring, controlling, and addicted to substance and alcohol abuse. This misrepresentation of mental health professionals by the media makes a person affected by mental illness reluctant in seeking for treatment (Freeman et al., 2001). The message that the public receives from this misrepresentation by the media is that it is not worth helping others.

Social Status when Media Reports on Mental Illness

When reporting on a person affected by mental illness, most mass media focus on their economic and social status. For those who are in the middle class and those of high rank, the media will report on their status and their affluence and give very little information concerning their mental state. This is different when reporting on those whose economic status is low; the media focus will be on their financial status, poverty, and its contribution to their mental illness. The media also connects some mental illnesses to the level of income of people. The media relates schizophrenia to poor people and depression to the middle class. Because of this kind of misrepresentation, the community tends to place a person affected by mental illness as not a part of the society or as an outcast or as either poor or rich (Olstead, 2002).

Notion That Some Cultures Are More Prone to Mental Illness in Comparison to Others

The mass media in their reports can indicate that people from a specific cultural background are more likely to develop certain types of mental illnesses in comparison to others. The reality is anyone is at a risk of developing mental illness.

Impact of Media Misrepresentation on Those Who Are Affected by Mental Illness

When the media represents the people affected by mental illness negatively, there is a negative impact on these people. One of the impacts is that these people are discriminated against by the society since they are seen to be different. The sick person rarely goes for treatment because of stigma. The various forms of media display mental illness in a way that increases stigma for those affected by mental illness.

Television usually depicts those who are affected by mental illness as being violent. In most television shows and movies, the people playing the character of a person affected by mental illness typically have no other identity apart from the one related to the illness. Thus, being sick mentally becomes their main character, and the illness becomes the only way of defining the person. In some television shows, most of the characters affected by mental illness kill another character in the show (Singorielli, 1989).

Also, on television, the individuals affected by mental illness are portrayed as being unproductive in the society. They are shown as people who live alone and have been rejected by their families and relatives. By the media isolating them, people affected by mental illness tend to feel inferior and unimportant (Olstead, 2002). With time, a person affected by mental illness starts to believe what the media says and how the public views them; they tend to think they are failures. The thought pattern of failure comes from the television shows where the characters playing the role of a person affected by mental illness acting in the play are depicted as failures. The result is that an ill person starts feeling and behaving as an outcast in the society.

Impact of Media Misrepresentation on the Public

Since the media mostly depict those who are people affected by mental illness as being violent, this makes the public fear them. The society tends to discriminate against those who are affected by mental illness. Children programmes on television also impact on how the public views those who are affected by mental illness. An example is a programme by the name *Beauty and the Beast*, where one character by the name Maurice is referred to as crazy and lunatic (Lawson & Fouts, 2004). The programme is aired on popular networks, such as ABC, Cartoon Network, and Nickelodeon. A large number of the characters are male, have no family, and are single. These programmes influence the children's way of thinking at an early age on how to treat those who are affected by mental illness. The public tends to interpret the actions of the male, single, and those living alone who behave differently from the rest of the society as being affected by mental illness because of the characters in the television shows.

Impact of Media Misrepresentation on Government Policies

When the media portrays those who are affected by mental illness as dangerous and violent, this influence the social policies made by the government. The social policies will aim more at containing and controlling those who are affected by mental illness, rather than having policies that can help in recovery. Adverse media reporting where those affected by mental illness are seen as being violent can result in policies and legislations where the sick person is forced to undergo treatment. Also, since the public would be living in fear of those affected by mental illness, there would be an increase of police power in the community because of the fear the people have (Rose, 1998).

According to Olstead (2002), Canadian newspapers stated that the resources which are meant for healthcare should be used to protect the community against those who are affected by mental illness. These funds should ideally be used in enhancing the mental health services, but because of the misrepresentation by the media concerning those affected by mental illness, the resources are directed at protecting the community against those affected by mental illness.

Examples of Media Reports Which Stigmatise against Mental Illness

There are various ways in which media stigmatise against those who are affected by mental illness. The media can do this either knowingly or unknowingly. Some examples of how media report can put a stigma on mental illness are through trivialising mental disorder and by misusing some medical terms, which extend the false impression that the public has towards mental illness. One of the names the media uses is the word *psycho*, which brings confusion between a psychopath, which is violence that is extreme, and psychosis, which means mental illness. The media also uses language which is demeaning; an example is the use of the words *psycho, schizo, lunatic* among other words. This kind of language puts a stigma on those who are affected by mental illness.

Media also reports using a language which victimises those who have mental illness. Some of the speeches which victimises those with mental illness is referring to them as victims or people suffering from mental illnesses. Another word which victimises those with mental illness is referring to them using their mental illness; an example is referring to someone having schizophrenia as schizophrenic. At times, during television interviews, the consent of the interviewee who has the mental illness is not requested. The media can also lack the right information on a particular mental illness and resort to reporting by use of myths.

Social Media's Negative Impact on Mental Illness

Social media includes Facebook, Twitter, Instagram among others. It has a significant influence on the public while reporting on the people who are affected by mental illness. There are various terms in connection to mental illness which people use on social media in relation to their day-to-day life stresses. The use of the words could be innocent but may have a negative impact on how the public views mental illness. The public may begin to take the various mental illnesses casually and view those with the illness as people who can quickly snap out of that state.

There are instances when people on social media use terms such as 'feeling schizo' to mean that they are feeling schizophrenic. The term *schizo* is used wrongly, which tends to reduce the seriousness of schizophrenia which is a mental disorder. The public starts to view those people affected by Schizophrenia as only being moody. This may make the society not to sympathise with people affected by schizophrenia because of the wrong portrayal through the social media platform.

Some social media users also term people affected by mental illness as 'retards', which is a derogatory term. Through the use of such a phrase, the public begins to view people affected by mental illness as being unintelligent. The public, rather than helping a sick individual to seek treatment, looks down on them and see an ill person as one who is beyond help.

On social media platforms, there is the abuse of the word *anorexia*, which is an eating and mental disorder. When women want to go on a diet to lose weight, they use phrases such as 'I am going anorexic'. This is a misrepresentation of those people battling anorexia as the public starts to look at the disorder as something one can quickly turn off without any form of treatment. The society begins to see anorexia as a diet and not an illness requiring treatment. Those who have anorexia, mostly the teenagers and adolescents, start to see their condition as being normal. Mental health professionals and therapists working with those affected by the disorder will have to do a lot in convincing the sick individual that what they are experiencing is not normal. The social media, by relating anorexia to a diet, makes those affected to deny the existence of any problem, which can be detrimental to their health.

There are also posts on social media regarding anxiety disorder, where people trivialise the illness. The person with the anxiety disorder is given a few steps to follow to get over the condition. Some of the steps provided on social media include the person being asked to take a deep breath and relax and have an internal monologue while repeating some phrases, such as 'It is okay'. Some social media posts also depict anxiety disorder sarcastically. This kind of social media posts, rather than helping an affected individual, makes their situation worse since some may try the suggestions given through social media but the disorder persists. The seriousness of the illness is trivialised through these posts. The public does not see the affected person as one who requires treatment.

The impressions given by social media regarding anxiety disorder makes the public not to empathise with those living with the condition. Social media posts from various people also provide suggestions on the kind of medication to take to deal with anxiety disorder. A particular type of drug can be portrayed as having no side effects and as a complete cure for the illness. This kind of information is misleading since medication alone is not enough to treat anxiety disorder; therapy is also necessary.

On some social media platforms, such as Facebook, the young people suffering from depression and other forms of mental illness can take away their lives since they feel like failures in comparison to their peers on Facebook who do not have the same illness. At times, when a person affected by mental illness posts something concerning their condition on social media, they become subjects of social media bullying or cyberbullying. The result of this is that the person may decide to end their lives. Also, the illness or disorder may become worse as they choose not to go for treatment so that they fit among their peers on social media.

How Social Media Can Positively Represent Mental Illness

Social media is a useful tool in educating the public about mental illness and reducing stigma against them. In comparison to printed information, social media is more effectual in changing the attitude of the public towards those who are affected by mental illness (Finkelstein et al., 2008). There are various ways in which social media can positively represent those who are affected by mental illness and reduce stigmatisation against them. There are multiple groups on social media sites where people with a particular kind of mental illness, such as depression, can share their experiences. People within the group share freely concerning what they go through regarding the illness. By doing this, they can conquer the fear of having to live with mental illness. They also advise one another, which is therapeutic.

Social media is helpful for those with mental illness since they can talk freely about issues that concern them and which they are unable to speak with their friends and family. Social media can be helpful in averting some disastrous effects of mental illness, such as taking away of lives. There are cases where a person affected by mental illness has put a post on social media on their intention to take away their life.

Online friends have been able to avert this by reaching out with love and support to the person.

YouTube, which is a social media platform, has been used by various people with severe mental illness, which include schizophrenia or bipolar disorder, to share their experiences with the illness. People with schizophrenia, bipolar disorder, or any other critical mental disorders can discuss the challenges they have faced and how they have overcome them. This becomes educative to those watching them and having the same condition. Through posting on social media, people affected by anxiety and obsessive-compulsive disorder can control some of the symptoms of the illness. Since the mind and attention of the person with the illness are active on social media, they may not have time to dwell on fearful or obsessive thoughts.

Some campaigns have been started on social media to help in sensitising the public concerning different mental illnesses and disorders. The campaigns assist in educating the public and in giving support to people who may be struggling with mental disorders. Since most people with mental illness rarely disclose their condition to friends, family, or colleagues, the campaigns aim at giving these people a listening ear. One such campaign which began in 2013 in New York is the 'I Will' campaign. The campaign mobilises people on various social media platforms to offer support to people with mental illness. Those with mental illness through the campaign get people in whom they can confide.

These campaigns also help in educating the public on the causes of mental illness so that the person affected may not be blamed for the cause of the illness. Some social sites permit people to share their feelings anonymously; this gives help to those who could be socially isolated and lonely. There are also some people who publicly share their struggles with a particular kind of mental illness. By doing this, others can learn on how to manage their mental illness and not be ashamed concerning their condition.

There is the provision of various educational materials on mental illness on social media sites. The materials are easily accessible, and this helps in increasing awareness concerning mental illness to both the public and the person who is affected by mental illness. Mental health practitioners also use social media to educate the public on mental illness, which can help in reducing stigmatisation to those who are affected by mental illness.

In Canada, *StigmaBusters* is a newsletter on the internet which the National Alliance for the Mentally Ill produces. The newsletter aims at portraying mental illness positively. The newsletter looks for positive stories in regard to mental illness in magazines, newspapers, and television and puts them in the newsletter.

Internet by the use of programmes which are web-based can be used to help reduce stigma which the mental health professionals face and educate those who are affected by mental illness and the public on various mental disorders. An example is the Blue Pages website that has information on depression; it targets people with depression and the public.

How the Mass Media Can Positively Represent Mental Illness

Though mass media and social media hurt those who are affected by mental illness through misrepresentation, there are things and tools which the media can use to help reduce stigma against these people. One of the ways is educating the public on mental health. An example is when newspapers and radio and television shows are used for events, such as the World Mental Health Day which help in educating the public. The media can also discuss the various causes of mental illness which are either environmental or biological, rather than putting the blame on the parents or the individual (Corrigan et al., 2005). This plays a significant role in changing the public's perception on those who are affected by mental illness as being responsible for their condition. Some of the ways and tools which the media can use to represent mental illness and reduce stigmatisation include the following:

Newspapers and Magazines

Newspapers are a valuable media tool that can be used to sensitise the public on mental illness. For example, newspapers can conduct campaigns with an aim of educating the society on the different kinds of mental illness and the symptoms which may indicate that a person has a mental disorder and the various forms of treatment available for various mental disorders. Beyond Blue is an example of a campaign done in Australia with the sole purpose of educating the public on anxiety and depression and lessening the stigma associated with the disorders. When newspapers feature stories on recovery for those previously had mental illness, there is a reduction of stigma towards the people affected by mental illness (Corrigan et al., 2013).

Television

Media can use entertainment programmes as a tool of education. Television shows whose characters portray people affected by mental illness as violent or dangerous should be replaced with shows where a person affected by mental illness is seen to be sick and not dangerous. One such television show is *Monk,* where the main character has obsessive-compulsive disorder (Hoffner & Cohen, 2012). The main character of this television series uses the disorder to accurately check aspects of crimes which are complicated and resolves them. The television show portrays obsessive-compulsive disorder positively, thus reducing stigma about the illness. The people who watch the show and have the disorder begin to view themselves positively and seek for treatment enthusiastically.

Another movie which depicts those who have mental illness positively is the movie by the name *As Good as It Gets,* where the main character has obsessive-compulsive disorder, who—through medication and therapy—wins the love of a woman. The movie depicts a person with this kind of disorder as one who can have relationships, have a family, and live a healthy life. The film manages to reduce the stigma by the public against those living with the obsessive-compulsive disorder and even raise the self-esteem of those living with the disorder.

Documentary Films

Other tools which the media can use to reduce stigma and communicate positively on mental illness are documentary films (Penn et al., 2003). By watching documentary films, the viewer can acquire more information concerning a particular mental illness. The result is that the public, through documentary films, would tend to respond more positively to those with mental illness. In comparison to movies which are fictional, documentary films provides more information to the public and helps in changing their attitude to the people affected by mental illness.

An example of the effectiveness of educating the public on mental illness through documentary films is a study conducted in Switzerland. According to Laroi and Van der Linden (2009), students who watched a documentary film on people with schizophrenia became accommodative to those with the disorder. The stigma and discrimination towards those with schizophrenia reduced after watching the documentary. In comparison to educating the public on schizophrenia, documentary films tend to change the society's view towards those with schizophrenia and other mental illnesses (Corrigan et al., 2007).

In 2007, the Scottish Mental Health Arts and Film Festival began. The primary purpose of the festival is to display the creative works of people with mental illness (Dingfelder, 2009). The festival incorporates competitions of documentaries or movies which realistically portray mental illness. The purpose of doing this is to raise awareness in the public concerning mental illness and educate the society. Schools can use educative movies on mental illness to teach the schoolgoing children on mental illness, causes, symptoms and on how to relate to those with mental illness.

Language

A language is also a tool which can be used to represent those with mental illness through media positively. Reporting whether through printed materials—such as newspapers, magazines, journals—television, or social media should be done by the use of 'people-first language.' Terms such as 'depressed people' or 'schizophrenic people' should be avoided. When reporting on a person with a certain mental illness, the right language should be 'a person affected by the bipolar disorder or schizophrenia' but not 'a schizophrenic person'. Other words that the media should avoid during reporting is referring to the person affected by mental illness as being a nut, crazy, psycho, or lunatic.

Methods of Reporting

The media should avoid negative stereotypes when referring to an individual affected by mental illness. Some of the stereotypes that the media should avoid are linking mental illness to violence, crime, and dangerousness. Images which portray people affected by mental illness as being unkempt and sinister should not be used by the media. This will help promote positive depiction of those with mental illness. Media should also avoid linking normal human behaviour, such as anger and sadness, to mental illness. The media should not connect mental illnesses to only a single cause since the causes of various mental disorders are many. By doing this, the public will tend to discriminate less those with mental illness together with their families and caregivers.

When reporting on an individual with mental illness, the media should ensure that the person has a mental illness diagnosis from a mental health professional to avoid giving wrong information. The next step is for the media to make sure that the information presented is authentic to avert providing incorrect information. There should be consideration of the right to privacy of the person. If the health of the person would be at stake by reporting on the mental illness, then the media should reconsider their decision. The report should aim at giving facts with no exaggerations. In case mentioning the individual's name would cause stigma, the media can look for alternatives by using a pseudonym in order to protect the person.

The media should report on mental illness as being preventable and recoverable. When media reports on mental illness as an illness where one cannot recover from, those with the illness tend to become hopeless. The reality is mental illness can be treated, and the person has a chance of recovery. When reporting on criminal or violent acts about a person who is affected by mental illness, the media should also include the possibility of recovery. Also, when reporting on a story on a specific mental illness, the media should involve a mental health professional to avoid giving erroneous information to the public.

In cases where the media needs to interview a person who has a mental illness, the individual's consent should first be granted. The interviewer should ensure the interviewee is comfortable. The interviewer should see the interviewee as a person and not an illness or a diagnosis. The place and time of interview should be convenient to the interviewee. The time given to answer the question should be enough since the person affected by the mental illness may be having physical or emotional pain while discussing their experience. The news reporter, while conducting the interview, should be sensitive to the needs of the interviewee by listening actively and watching the non-verbal cues. The media should avoid interviewing an individual displaying psychotic behaviour and who is not in touch with reality until the person has recovered.

There are occasions when a person affected by mental illness can resort to taking away their lives. In such instances, if the media needs to report on the issue of death through suicide, they need to observe some critical factors. Some of the elements they should observe include the avoidance of using pictures or photographs of the family and friends who are grieving after the person has taken away their life. Images of the grieving family can cause someone planning to take away their lives to do so as a way of getting attention from their family and friends.

Media should also not give details on how the person took away their lives and on the location where the act took place. This helps in protecting those vulnerable from doing the same. Media should also avoid depicting taking away of one's life as an act of heroism since this is not the reality. On both newspapers and televisions, death through suicide should not be used in headlines. The media should avoid myths during reporting on people who take away their lives. Some of the myths include 'cowards are the ones who take away their lives'. The media should aim at providing help to those who may be intending to take away their lives.

When reporting on people with various kinds of addiction which may involve drug and substance abuse, the media should not portray the person as being weak. They should give facts regarding the habit. One of the facts is addiction can be a result of genetic and environmental factors. The media should also emphasise that addictions are mental disorders and the person with the addiction is sick and in need of treatment from a mental health professional. By doing this, the stigma against those with substance and drug addictions tends to reduce in the society. The person is also able to see their need for treatment.

The media should adhere to the code of conduct while reporting on mental illnesses. Media can be a powerful tool in removing stigma which is associated with those who have mental illnesses.

CHAPTER 3

Stigma And Mental Illness - Part II

In chapter 2, we looked at the definition of stigma, the two types of stigma, and the media and its impact on stigmatisation to those who have mental illness. In chapter 2, the misrepresentation of mental illness by the media was discussed at length, and the ways in which the media can positively represent people with mental illness were looked into.

In chapter 3, we will look at how stigma brings the fear of rejection and loss of identity to those with mental illness. Various cultures and their approaches to stigma in connection to those with mental illness and how people with mental illness resort to self-medication to avoid stigma will also be subjects of this chapter.

Rejection as a Result of Stigma towards People with Mental Illness

When a person realises that they have been affected by mental illness, the first thing that happens to the person is the fear of being rejected. Most people affected by mental illness feel lonely most of the time because of the feeling that they cannot interact with other people as these people may be judging them because of the illness. Those affected by mental illness live in fear of rejection and are afraid to face the world. By withdrawing from the society, the society also withdraws from them. This person may want to have social contact with family and friends, but in most instances, because of the fear of rejection, they may not try to reach out to their family or even their friends. A person affected by mental illness may avoid other people to protect themselves against rejection.

Because of the stigma associated with mental illness, those affected by any mental disorder may fear rejection because of their condition. The fear may come from the fact that the person may have witnessed a person affected by mental illness undergoing rejection. Rather than going through the rejection, the person may prefer pushing people away, finding it easier to be alone rather than suffer rejection. The individual may push away people unwillingly because of the fear of what will happen in case they are rejected.

Anytime the person may want to form any kind of relationship, the question that comes to their mind is 'Will people reject me because of the mental illness?' This hinders the person from pursuing any opportunity in their lives. Since the individual expects rejection, they may avoid interacting with other people or forming any lasting relationship. A person affected by mental illness, because of the fear of rejection from the society, may avoid connecting with those around them. The fear of rejection makes availability of resources and treatment to the person a challenge since the person has alienated themselves from the community and may not be able to access the resources (Overton & Medina, 2008). There are various areas in which the person affected by mental rejection may fear rejection. They include having social relationships among other areas while seeking for employment.

The Fear of Rejection and the Workplace

An individual who has been affected by mental illness may fear disclosing their status to their colleagues at work so that they may not be rejected. A person may fear that by disclosing the mental illness, their colleagues may avoid them, and they end up becoming the objects of gossip in the office. A person may also fear not being considered for promotion because of the illness; thus, they may not ask for the promotion for fear of their request being turned down. An individual affected by mental illness may also be reluctant to apply for a job which they are qualified for because of the fear of their application being rejected as a result of the mental illness.

There are times when an individual may need time off to attend therapy or get treatment. The person may be afraid to request for days off in case the person in charge asks the reason for their absence. The person affected by mental illness may not want to disclose the reason for their absence for fear of rejection, which causes more health problems caused by lack of treatment. The individual is also afraid of being misunderstood by both the employer and colleagues in the workplace. The misunderstanding comes because of the fact the person at times may behave differently from the other colleagues. For example, some treatment for a person affected by schizophrenia can cause them to have tremors; this may cause them to fear looking for employment to avoid being stigmatised because of their condition. A mentally affected person would rather tell employers that they served time in jail than they have been hospitalised in a psychiatric facility (SAMHSA, 2003)

The Fear of Rejection and Social Relationship

A person affected by mental illness may fear disclosing their status to family and friends to avoid being rejected (Overton & Medina, 2008). The individual needs social relationships since they help in giving support during the hard times. Because of the stigma and discrimination which is associated with mental illness, the person, when starting a romantic relationship, may hide their status to avoid being rejected. Another reason of fearing rejection in forming a romantic relationship is because mental health professionals and caregivers usually discourage romantic relationships for a person who is affected by mental illness. This is because those affected by mental illness may be in a position to manage the challenges that can come in the relationship.

The individual may fear disclosing their status to the other person since the other person may begin to view them through their illness and not as a person. In some countries, such as China, mental illness is ground for divorce. The person affected by mental illness may be reluctant to get into marriage to avoid divorce. Those already in marriage and are affected by mental illness may opt to leave the marriage for fear of rejection from their spouses. Also, in marriage, the spouse who is not affected by a mental illness may tend to limit the interaction the other spouse has with the children. Because of this, the spouse affected by mental illness may hide their status for fear of being rejected by the children. In family relationships, an individual can be reluctant to talk about their illness to avoid being seen as a burden in the family since this might bring rejection to them. A person affected by mental illness can also hide their condition from friends because of the fear of friends leaving them.

The Fear of Rejection at School

Schoolgoing children and adolescents affected by mental illness may fear rejection from their peers and opt not to go to school. Some of the things which may cause them to fear attending school are the inability to concentrate in school, the challenge of meeting deadlines, the inability to handle noise and large crowds, and the challenge of making new friends. These factors can make the school going children opt out of school.

Steps on How to Overcome the Fear of Rejection

There are things which a person affected by a mental illness can do to overcome the fear of rejection. Some of the steps which the person—or in case of children, their parents—can do to conquer the fear of rejection.

Changing the Thought Pattern

A person who has the fear of rejection should learn to have positive thoughts towards themselves and their circumstances. At times, the person may be concerned so much about what other people think about their status, yet this may not be the reality. The person should substitute their pessimistic thoughts with optimistic or positive thoughts; the person should understand that everyone gets rejected in their lives at one time or another and realise that not all people are likely to reject them because of mental illness.

Overcoming the Fear of Rejection by Facing It

Adverse or negative thoughts come as a result of fear. An individual, because of fear, may opt to do nothing and take no action. By avoiding any action, the negative thinking makes the fear of rejection worse. This person should act despite what they feel and think. They can begin by taking a few steps out of their safety zones and by risking rejection from the society the person is, on their way to overcoming the fear of rejection. There is a likelihood that the person will not face rejection, and even if they do, the consequence may not be as dire as the individual had earlier thought.

The parents, whose children fear rejection at school because of the effects of mental illness, should communicate with their children in regard to the fear of rejection. The parent can help the child focus on their strengths which may include the child's willingness to help others, their good sense of humour, their creativity, and the fact that they may be fast to learn new things. By doing this, the child will learn to accept themselves and not fear what other people say concerning the fact that they have been affected by mental illness. Overcoming or defeating the fear of rejection for a person affected by mental illness may take time, but the individual should persist and not give up.

Stigma and Social Affiliation

In the Western culture, stigmatisation of those affected by mental illness is extensive (Crisp et al., 2001). Those people affected by mental illness suffer most from isolation by the society. A person may desire contact with family and friends, but because of the stigma attached to mental illness, the society may refuse to accommodate the person. A person who is mentally affected tends to not interact with people in the community because of the stigma which is associated with mental illness. When the society views those affected by mental illness as being dangerous, they tend to avoid them because of fear (Corrigan et al., 2001). Thus, because of the social distance, a person affected by mental illness may not be able to form any social relationship.

By lacking social contact, a mentally affected individual becomes lonely, which takes a toll on their health. The person can result to substance and alcohol abuse, which further worsens their condition. Social exclusion can result in the person living in poverty since they earn less income since they lack employment opportunities as a result of their mental illness (Jenkins et al., 2008). Social exclusion can also be a result of lack of a productive activity, which comes from the fact that the person may have no education. The person may have discontinued their education because of their mental illness. The individual can also suffer from exclusion in the workplace from both their colleagues and employer.

An individual affected by mental illness suffers from lack of social relationships since the public does not want to live in the same neighbourhood with them. The person is unlikely to take part in leisure activities because of the nature of the illness, discrimination, and level of income. They may be excluded from participating in civic activities; this is because of the lack of information in social policies on how to involve people affected by mental illness in the making of local and national decisions. According to Rethink (2010), people affected by mental sickness cannot serve in juries.

People affected by mental sickness suffer exclusion from health services. This results on early deaths. For example, people affected by schizophrenia or bipolar disorder die younger than the general population. These people are also at risk of developing hypertension, diabetes, obesity, heart ailments, and cancer in comparison to the general public (DRC, 2006). The healthcare providers may not take a person affected by mental illness seriously when they complain of symptoms related to other ailments as this may be taken to be a product of their imagination.

The lack of social affiliation can hinder recovery for a person affected by mental illness. The diagnosis can cause the person to alienate themselves, making the outcome of the diagnosis worse. The result for the isolation is the person developing low self-esteem, resulting into a vicious cycle of conquering individual and social problems. Isolation leads to social stigma and withdrawal, slowing down the recovery process.

Ways of Inclusion for Those Affected by Mental Illness

The people affected by mental illness should be able to participate and give back to the society. There are various ways in which people affected by mental illness can be included in the society. Some of the ways include the following:

Involving the Caregivers in the Inclusion Programme

According to Mental Health Council of Australia (2005), caregivers contribute much of their time caring for the individual affected by mental illness. This causes a strain on them; thus, they should be part of any inclusion programme. Including the caregivers in the society reduces the risk of them developing problems in their mental health and being unable to take care of their loved ones who already are affected by mental illness.

Having Access to Services Which Are Community-Based

There should be agencies within the community to give rehabilitation services to a person who has been affected by mental illness. The focus of the rehabilitation is to treat the effects of the mental illness. The process may take an extended period since the person will have to recover from self-stigma, adverse effects of lacking employment, loss of opportunities among other issues (Ridgway, 2001). In community-based services, the person is provided with facilities where they can have leisure time and be able to connect with other members of the society.

Having Access to Health Services

Patients affected by mental sicknesses and in need of care for an extended period can access clinical services within the community rather than in the hospitals offering psychiatric services. This will help the community to be a part of the patient's recovery process. During treatment, the patient can also enjoy activities which are recreational. With time, because of the support from the society, the patient can cease depending on the psychiatric services (Rog, 2004).

Having Access to Employment

When seeking for employment, these people meet many barriers which include stigma and discrimination from employers and scarcity of workplaces which can accommodate their needs. Socially including the person affected by mental illness in employment can help in improving their health. Obtaining employment can help the person's self-esteem become higher, symptoms related to the mental illness tend to decrease, and their sense of self-worth also increases (Frost et al., 2002). By being employed, the individual gets included in the community, which enables them to take an active role in the society (Waghorn & Llyod, 2005).

Employment can help in the recovery process for an individual affected by mental illness as the person feels a part of the society. Most people who are affected by mental illness desire to work as they regard it as being helpful in their recovery (Waghorn & Llyod, 2005).

Stigma and Loss of Identity

Identity refers to feelings, characteristics, and images which a person acknowledges as being a part of themself. Identity can be classified into social, personal, and ego identity. Social identity is where people who do not know the person on an individual level tend to define the individual depending on what they have heard concerning them. Personal identity, on the other hand, comes from the life story of the individual. Ego identity, on the other hand, means the way in which a person establishes their own identity and how they identify themselves.

People affected by mental illness tend to lose their identity after the diagnosis; an example is when someone diagnosed with schizophrenia describes themself as a computer that needs rebooting (Gould et al., 2005). These people also feel that they have lost their former or previous self. The person also feels they have lost their self-esteem and respect, especially when seeking for employment (Basset et al., 2001). Hospitalisation may also cause the person to feel as though they have no control over their lives. Most people affected by mental illness experience the loss of self-confidence due to stigma (Browne et al., 2008).

The person may experience challenges in activities which they previously performed with ease. This can result in the person's view of themself changing (Wittman & Keshavan, 2007). Becoming a patient in a psychiatric hospital can become the person's identity, where the person sees themself as a patient, or because of the nature of the mental illness, the person begins to believe they are someone else. Loss of identity for the mentally sick can also occur since their personal observations cannot be relied upon, thus forcing them to get a new definition of their identity and their expectations of themselves (Farone & Pickens, 2007).

Self-stigma, where the person affected by mental illness believes the society's perception concerning those affected by mental illness through their personal experience or through what other people experience, can have an impact on their identity. Self-stigma lowers the person's self-esteem and capability in attaining their goals (Overton & Medina, 2008). Loss of identity can cause the person to grieve in secret because of being misunderstood by the community (Young, Bailey, & Rycroft, 2004).

Ways to Recover from Loss of Identity for Those Affected by Mental Illness

There are various things which a person affected by mental illness can do in order to gain back their self-identity. They include the following:

By Working or Being in Employment

The recovery of the identity of the individual affected by mental illness can be enhanced through resuming work for the person who was previously employed or looking for employment for the person who was not employed before the occurrence of the mental illness. By engaging in employment, the person gets the feeling that they are like the rest of the people. Working helps the person reduce their financial or emotional dependence on other people.

The person may have experienced extended periods of hospitalisation and isolation; by being employed, they are able to move away from the identity of being a patient to that of being a worker. Also, through employment, the person feels needed since their absence is noted by colleagues and employers and by being a part of an organisation. In the workplace, the person is able to focus on work-related issues and not on their status in regard to the mental illness.

Employment provides financial independence which enables the mentally affected person to engage in social activities in the society. This helps in regaining their self-identity. Through financial independence, the person's self-esteem increases as they are able to make decisions on their own.

Through Establishing Relationships

The people that are around an individual affected by mental illness play a key role in helping them gain their lost identity. Their family, friends, and mental health professionals should value the person as a human being who is unique. The people around them should also trust the credibility of what the person says and learn to trust them, especially during the recovery process. Listening to what the person says should be done in a non-judgemental way, especially when they talk about their future which may look uncertain at that moment. The person may be unwilling to set goals in regard to their lives; the people around them can encourage the person to set goals and strive to attain them. By doing this, the person will gain back their lost identity and not regard themselves as being only patients.

Cultures in Relation to Stigma Associated with Mental Illness

Culture can be defined as the behaviours and norms of a society; it can also be defined as the beliefs and customs of a particular group of people. Different cultures have different perspectives on mental illness, which influence the attitudes they have towards those affected by mental illness and mental illness in general. Culture influences how mental illness is viewed and what kind of treatment is administered to those affected. Religion and culture influence the beliefs which people hold on the causes of mental illness. These beliefs have an impact on the stigma which the people who are affected by mental illness experience.

Some cultures stigmatise all mental illnesses, while others stigmatise a few illnesses only. People who are racially and ethnically regarded as minorities have a different way of handling mental illness in comparison to people from other cultures. Culture influence how patients express the symptoms of mental illness, how willing they are in seeking treatment, and how they manage the illness.

Patients from different cultures often describe the symptoms they have differently; for example, patients from an Asian background will only tell the mental health professional about their somatic symptoms but not the emotional symptoms which they could be experiencing (Lin & Cheung, 1999). Another example is when ethnic and racial minorities in the United States, in comparison to the whites, rarely seek for treatment in regard to their mental health. These minority groups may also delay treatment for mental illness until the symptoms become severe or unbearable. These people tend to rely more on traditional methods of treatment, such as traditional healers and prayers, because of the fear of formal treatment methods, which to them are dominated by people from a different race.

Stigma Associated with Mental Illness in the African Latino Culture

The Latino community is an ethnic group in America; it is the largest group among the ethnic minorities. The community includes people from Mexico, the Caribbean, and countries from Central America. The Latinos are religious people, having a large number of the population identify themselves with Christianity. They also hold other religious beliefs, such as Curanderismo, Espiritismo, and Santeria. The belief of Curanderismo originated from the humoral medication from Greek and Judeo-Christian traditions on healing. Curanderismo believes that illness is caused by either natural or supernatural forces or both. The healing methods can be supernatural through spiritual or physical purification (Luna, 2003).

Santeria, which is practiced by Cubans, is a mixture of Catholic and African beliefs. The methods of healing in this practice include casting out evil spirits, using magic medicines and amulets, and sacrificing animals. Espiritismo is a belief system which the people from Puerto Rico use; they believe that sickness is a result of fluids from a person's spirit and those of the dead who are close to the person. In order for the person to obtain healing, prayer is conducted; there are also personal and house purifications (Baez & Hernandez, 2001).

The Latinos also have the belief in *locura*, which refers to an acute kind of psychosis. A person with *locura* has symptoms of being incoherent, having hallucinations which are visual, and being violent. The Latinos differentiate between an individual who is *un loco tranquilo* and *un loco violent*, which means a person affected by mental illness who is quiet and one who is violent, respectively. There is more stigma associated with the person who is violent than the one who is quiet. These cultures among the Latinos influence how they perceive those who are affected by mental illness among them.

Factors Determining the Stigma Associated with Mental in the Latino Society

Mental illness is referred to as *loco*, which is a stigmatising term against those affected by mental illness. The caregivers and family of the person affected by mental illness tend to socially distance themselves from the affected individual. There are various factors among the Latino community which determine how the community perceives the people affected by mental illness among them, these factors include the following:

Experiences Associated with Migration

The Latinos who migrate to America experience stress associated with relocation since there is an emphasis for them to live independently. Some of the Latinos tend to believe that migration causes dementia. Migration brings culture shock since they experience a different way of living from what they are used to since back home, cohesion within the family is of great value, which is not the case in

America. The contrast in the values between their traditional culture and those that they experience in the United States can bring stress, resulting to mental sickness.

Mental illness attracts a lot of stigma among the Latinos; thus, they may be unwilling to seek treatment. At times, mental illness is linked to being weak, being violent, and having no control. Because of the fear of rejection by their family, a person affected by mental illness may opt to hide their condition.

The Kind of Treatment Given to Those Affected by Mental Illness

People affected by mental illness fear taking medications from psychiatric hospitals since they perceive the medication as being addictive. Another reason the person may fear taking the medication is because they are afraid being seen as people who cannot control their symptoms, which can cause them to suffer stigma. By taking the medication, the person is viewed as weak and one who cannot control their symptoms. By not taking medication, the severity of mental illness among those affected becomes worse.

Ways in Which Stigma for Those Affected by Mental Illness Can Be Overcome

In order to reduce the stigma associated with mental illness among the African Latinos, there are various things which can be done. Among them are the following:

Increasing Services to Those Affected by Mental Illness

Increase of accessibility of services can help reduce the stigma associated with people affected by mental illness since the Latinos will not have to resort to informal methods of treatment. Since they are religious, the programmes for mental health should include religious values to make the services more appealing to those affected by mental sickness.

Upgrading the Communication between the Client and the Therapist

By training more Latinos on mental health, the people affected by mental illness would be able to access mental health services as there will be no language barrier because both the mental health provider and the client will be speaking the same language. In facilities where there is a language barrier, interpreters should be made available.

Incorporating Culture in the Mental Health Programmes

The Latinos are people deeply rooted in their culture; an example is that they believe in the supernatural through spiritual or physical purification as a method of treatment for those affected by mental illness (Luna, 2003). By incorporating culture in the mental health programmes, the Latinos would be able to identify more with the method of treatment. For the mental health professionals to be effective, they should learn the culture of the people whom they are giving treatment. Also, the treatment method should be sensitive to the culture of the Latinos, and the patient should be enlightened on what to expect during treatment.

Stigma Associated with Mental Illness in the Asian Culture

In Asia, talking about mental illness is a challenge since it is considered a taboo subject; those affected by mental illness are considered weak, guilty of their status, and a shame to the society (Kishore et al., 2011). Many Asian countries, especially those that are in South Asia, live as a community, making it necessary to maintain the image of the society. When a person is affected by mental illness, the community's image is tainted; thus, the person is expected to hide their condition to not tarnish the society's image (Amri & Bemak, 2012). In most countries in Asia, mental illness is seen as a form of punishment or judgement of the ancestors' wrongdoing, which extends to the current generation.

Because of the shame associated with mental illness, few people would want any interaction or social affiliation with the affected person. In order to avoid being labelled as an outcast, the person may avoid seeking for treatment, or in case the treatment had started, the person may discontinue (Corrigan & Kosyluk, 2014, p. 40). In Asia, the stigma associated with mental illness causes the individual to delay treatment to avoid people from knowing their condition. By the time the person looks for treatment from a mental health professional, the illness becomes hard to treat, and the recovery process is often slow.

In South Asia, mental illnesses are linked to the possession by spirits, the lack of faith, and the evil eye. These become deterrents to seeking medical care for the person who is affected (Amri & Bemak, 2012, p. 50). When the mental illness is perceived to have originated from an 'evil eye', the blame is put on the person with the 'evil eye' and not the affected person, thus viewing the individual affected by mental sickness as only a victim. Seeing these people as victims creates empathy from the community, which makes them to be viewed as those who cannot recover (Roe et al., 2014). When the person is seen as an object, pity in the community brings with it the benevolent kind of stigma.

In Vietnam, the traditional setting of the man being the only one who can make decisions in a home is still maintained. In this cultural setting, if a woman develops mental illness, the husband is the only one who can decide if—or when and where—the wife is to get treatment.

In China and India, families of people affected by mental illness are seen as being socially polluted (Rao et al., 2014, p. 287). This causes both the family and the affected person to hide the condition from the society. The family does this to avoid stigma and discrimination from the public. At times, family members, because of embarrassment, tend to distance themselves from the person. For parents who are affected by mental illness, their children are viewed as being 'genetically polluted', (Moses, 2014). This causes the children to be stigmatised against in the society.

The Chinese society views mental illness as a cause by the anger of the gods or as a result of a demonic possession. Since the illness is linked to shame, the affected person tries to hide the illness or tends to live in denial to rid the family of the stigma of mental illness. The Chinese community strongly resists seeking mental healthcare services for those who are mentally ill and opts to use somatisation, special diets, herbs, and traditional medication in treating mental illness.

China, which is in Asia, have various beliefs or myths in connection to mental illness. One of the myths is the belief that being mentally sick means the person is crazy, which to some people means having a severe mental illness, such as schizophrenia. Another myth is the belief that people who are mentally ill are more violent in comparison to other people, yet many of the people who commit crimes which are violent are rarely mentally affected. Because of this myth, people affected by mental illness in China are usually hospitalised against their will.

The Chinese society also believes that mental illness is a Western experience. This belief is not true since mental illnesses affect people from all cultures. The fourth belief that the Chinese society associates with mental illness is that people who have psychiatric issues or problems need to work more diligently. This belief is associated with depression, where the person may be unable to work. The Chinese society believes that this person needs to work harder to rid themself of depression. The Chinese society believes that mental illness is often a result or consequence of a person's misconduct or wrongdoing in their previous life (Pescolido et al., 2013). This community also believes that mental illnesses have no cure or treatment. The opposite is true; most mental illnesses and disorders can be easily treated and managed.

These myths or beliefs in the Chinese society result in many people affected by mental illness hiding their condition because of the fear of experiencing stigma from the community. Since mental illness is a taboo topic in the Chinese community, those affected are reluctant to seek for medical help to avoid being labelled as crazy. The affected person tends to feel hopeless since they are not acting in the way which the society expects of them.

In many Asian countries, the permission of the family is required by the mental health professional for them to treat the person affected by mental illness. The purpose for this is for the health professional to understand the cultural views of the patient's family concerning the origin of the illness and their expectations in regard to treatment. During treatment, the patient rarely says what they feel or think as the mental healthcare provider is regarded as the one in authority. Culture hinders the patient from giving their views to the healthcare provider as the physician is the authority and the patient's role is to only listen.

Ways to Reduce Stigma Associated with Mental Illness in Asia

There are various ways in which the stigma related to mental illness can be reduced. They include the following:

Training More Nurses on Mental Healthcare

In China, nurses have minimal training on how to deal with people affected by mental illness, which has largely contributed to stigmatising the mentally ill (Rameela, 2004). By training more nurses on mental healthcare, the stigma towards mental illness and the people affected will reduce as the nurses will view those affected as ill people in need of treatment. The nursing staff in the course of their duties should come into contact with people affected by mental illness to reduce the stigma. The training programmes should be customised depending on the attitude and knowledge level of the nurses for them to be effective. Nurses can also come up with activities whose aim is to sensitise the public on mental health issues to reduce the stigma associated with mental illness.

Breaking the Silence on Mental Illness

In most Asian countries, mental illness is rarely talked about; it is a taboo subject. The people affected by mental illness and those who have recovered can end the stigma and break the silence by sharing their experiences publicly. The media can be helpful in ending the stigma by inviting these people to share about mental illness challenges, available treatment methods, and how a person affected by mental illness should be viewed in the society.

Legislation

Laws which are anti-discriminatory can help in ending stigma which people affected by mental illness face. These laws can help in protecting the affected person and their family from any form of violence from the public. An example of one of these laws is the mental health law in China, which was published in 10 June 2011, with an aim of protecting patients against forceful hospitalisation. The laws also aims at ensuring transparency during the patient's treatment. The various legislations will help in preventing the taking away of life by people who are affected by mental illness because of the shame they suffer as a result of the illness.

Educating the Public on the Causes of Mental Illnesses

In many Asian countries, mental illness is viewed as a punishment from the gods or as an inheritance due to the misconduct of the ancestors or as a cause of witchcraft, magic, evil eye, or bad omen. Because of these cultural beliefs, most Asian communities resort to informal treatment methods, mostly from traditional healers. To change these cultural beliefs, the public needs to be taught on the causes and treatment methods of various mental illnesses; this will reduce the stigma associated with mental illness as the public will view the illness as being treatable. Pseudoscience is a huge opportunity lost, causing more harm than good to our society (Stanovich, 2013).

Reducing Stigma through the Use of Documentary Films

Documentary films are a major tool which can help reduce the stigma which comes as a result of mental illness. By watching the film, the public can get more information concerning mental illness. Since most of the documentary films feature people in real life, the society can identify with the story. An example of such a film in South Asia is the *Unbroken Glass*, where a young man by the name Dinesh Sabu, whose parents died as a result of taking away their lives, talks about taking away of lives and schizophrenia. This has helped in breaking the silence on these two mental illnesses.

Stigma Associated with Mental Illness in the Australian Culture

Australia is home to people of diverse cultures; people from Africa, Europe, Asia, Pacific islands all make their home in Australia. There are also indigenous Australians and migrants who do not speak English. These different groups of people have various cultures and beliefs which directly influence their views on mental illnesses.

One of the beliefs associated with mental illness in Australia is that only a few people get affected by mental illness; this is untrue since mental illness is common in Australia. Another belief that is held in Australian culture is that personal weakness causes mental illness; this is not a fact since mental illness is not a result of a defect of an individual's character (Reavley & Jorm, 2011). An example is when a person affected by depression is seen as being weak and few employers would be willing to employ the person (Reavley & Jorm, 2011). Mental illness is caused by various factors which include genetic or hereditary, environmental, biological, and social factors. The Australian society also believes people affected by mental illness never recover; thus, mental illness is viewed as a life sentence. This is false since most people affected by mental illness recover and live a productive life. Also, some individuals experience a single episode of the illness and recover completely. This myth is also not true as there are many treatment methods available which help the affected person manage the symptoms and recover.

Some of the people in the Australian culture believe that all mental disorders and illnesses are similar. This is only a myth as mental illnesses are many and are differentiated by the symptoms which the person exhibits. Also, one type of mental illness may have different symptoms depending on the individual. For example, one person affected by schizophrenia may hear voices or experience hallucinations, while a different person with the same diagnosis may not experience this.

Another belief is that a person affected by mental illness is able to get out of the illness on their own; this is untrue as mental illness cannot be treated by a person's own strength or will power. It needs professional healthcare. In Australia, people affected by mental illness are regarded as being violent (McGinty et al., 2013). The media is the major culprit of promoting this view, and since Australians are ardent media users, this has a negative impact on how they treat those affected by mental illness. The fact is people affected by mental illness usually are victims of being hurt by others; they are not more violent than the rest of the people in the society. Because of the misrepresentation by the media, those affected by mental illness, at times, resort to taking away their lives.

The Australian culture also hold the belief that people who are affected by mental illness should be kept in psychiatric hospitals. When the person affected by mental illness gets the right treatment, the individual is able to live in the community independently; thus, there is no need of keeping them in a hospital. These myths and cultural beliefs cause the public to avoid the person affected by mental illness, which cause them to suffer stigma in the society (Morgan et al., 2011).

Another myth associated with mental illness in Australia is that there are groups of people who are more prone to mental illness than others; this is not a fact as any person can have mental illness. Stigma towards mental illness in Australia hinders the affected person from getting a home in comparison to the general population. These people are, at times, forced to live in unsafe houses which are substandard (Australian Bureau of Statistics, 2009). The health professionals also stigmatise people affected by mental illness, where on reporting to the health practitioner concerning their symptoms, the person gets dismissed.

Ways of Reducing Stigma towards Mental Illness in the Australian Culture

There are various measures which have taken or done in Australia to help in the reduction of the stigma which those affected by mental illness face, but still, more needs to be done. Some more of the measures include the following:

Educating the Media on Accurate Representation of Mental Illness

The Mindframe National Media Initiative in Australia helps in training and sensitising the media on ways in which they need to represent mental illness correctly. The initiative helps in providing accurate information concerning various mental illnesses to the media. The Universities of Melbourne and the University of Canberra have helped in providing information and monitoring the media in regard to mental illness. With the information which they acquire, the media can help in educating the society on the fact that there are different kinds of mental illnesses. Also, one can recover from mental illness, and it is not a life sentence. By doing this, the media will be helping in fighting the stigma associated with mental illness in the Australian culture.

Reducing Stigma through Policies

There are various legislations and policies that have been put in place in Australia to help in lessening the stigma towards mental illness. One of the policies is the National Mental Health Policy, whose aim is to lower the effects of the problems which arise as a result of mental illness and the stigma which comes with the illness.

Another initiative which has helped in reducing the stigma towards mental illness is the beyondblue initiative, whose purpose is to raise the awareness on anxiety and depression, which are mental illnesses, to the public. The initiative has an objective of lowering the stigma associated with anxiety and depression. The beyondblue initiative has also helped in the reduction of stigma in the workplace from both the employer and the colleagues of the person affected by mental illness. Also, it has helped reduce the discrimination which people affected by depression and anxiety experience in the society by supporting change of attitudes towards these people.

Having Direct Contact with the Person Affected by Mental Illness

Coming into contact with the person affected by mental illness can help reduce the stigma that the public has towards the illness. The media can help by interviewing people who have recovered or are in the process of recovery from different mental illnesses. The media should avoid interviewing a person who is unwell or have not started their recovery process since this may influence the public adversely. These people can share their challenges and their recovery process; by doing this, some of the myths held in the Australian culture that one cannot recover from mental illness will dissipate.

Increasing Funding towards Mental Health through the Government

Increasing the funding given towards mental health will help improve the level of quality of services given to people affected by mental illness. By the individual receiving treatment, the quality of their life will improve, and the symptoms of the illness will become manageable, leading to the reduction of the stigma associated with the illness.

The Impact of Cognitive Closure on Mental Illness

Cognitive closure means the human desire or need to terminate or end any uncertainty. Human beings look for answers for uncertain or ambiguous situations because of the need for closure. There are benefits which are realised once a person secures or gets closure concerning a certain matter. An individual usually determines the level of the need for cognitive closure, depending on their personal traits. The need for closure is the desire which an individual has to have clear-cut answers; the answers need not be accurate. This need influences how a person behaves or responds to different situations.

Different circumstances may provoke the need for closure; some of these circumstances includes being under pressure to make fast decisions where thinking or working on the situation may not be pleasant. Another circumstance which can provoke the need for closure is when a person is handling tasks which are monotonous or boring or being in environments which are not comfortable, for example, being in an extremely cold or hot environment. A person may not see the need for closure when they derive pleasure from the task or when the answer to the task is wrong.

There are people whose need for closure is high, and they favour predictability and order. These people also have a closed mind and are able to make decisions; they also do not like any uncertainties. People whose need for closure rate is low come up with ideas more easily and are creative; these people, though having their views, consider diverse opinions.

People with a high need for closure view people who seem different from the rest of the society in a negative way. The presence of a high need for closure results in bias in choosing the information which is relevant and that needs to be attended. The high need of closure brings bias in judging and assessing of information and in considering information in the process of making decisions.

The need for closure usually brings with it the desire to have fast answers and to hold on to them. This need makes the person pay attention to the information received initially, and the individual is unlikely to change even when there is more evidence in regard to the information they have. The person interprets situations based on the information which was received initially without the use of other alternatives but through the use of stereotypes.

The need for closure results in lack of empathy since this may pose as a challenge to the judgement which the person holds. This need may cause an individual not to tolerate people who hold different views or beliefs regarding a certain situation or subject.

Components of Cognitive Closure

Cognitive closure comprises five elements, namely, being uncomfortable with ambiguity, desiring or needing predictability, predisposing towards order, being decisive, and having a closed mind (Webster & Kruglanski, 1994).

The first component is where the person is not comfortable with ambiguity. The individual views ambiguity as a risk to cognitive closure (Webster & Kruglanski, 1994). For an individual whose need for cognitive closure is high, the person may look for answers to lessen the uneasiness that comes with uncertainty or ambiguity.

The second component for cognitive closure is the desire or yearning for predictability or the capability to foretell the future, where the knowledge gained can be depended upon in various situations without deviation (Webster & Kruglanski, 1994). The people whose need for closure is high yearn for predictability in comparison to people whose need for closure is low.

The third component for cognitive closure favours or prioritises structure and order. Individuals whose need for closure is high prefer having order and structure in their environment in order to lessen anxiety when making decisions (Thompson et al., 2001).

The fourth component is being decisive, which means being able to make decisions. Individuals with a high need for closure are able to make decisions since they desire to arrive at a closure on the subject (Webster & Kruglanski, 1994). The people whose need for closure is low, on the other hand, may not be able to make decisions since they have no desire to arrive at a closure for a particular subject.

The fifth component of cognitive closure is having a closed mind; this is a state where a person is not willing to have their opinion challenged by different opinions or with information that is not consistent with what is generally acceptable.

Situations Where a Person Can Deviate from Their Need for Cognitive Closure

There are circumstances where people whose need for cognitive closure is low may look for cognitive closure. An example is when the person is mentally exhausted or is under time constraints. The individual with a high cognitive-closure need can keep away from cognitive closure if they are delighted on thinking concerning a particular subject. The fear of being adversely assessed by others can influence an individual's need for cognitive closure (Chirumbolo et al., 2005).

Cognitive Closure in Relation to Stigma Associated with Mental Illness

According to postmodernism, absolute truth does not exist, only different interpretations of the truth. Though the lay people believe that it exists, realities are usually socially constructed. An example of socially constructed realities is a man and a woman from two different backgrounds coming together to start a society. At the beginning, in order to live in harmony, they come up with habits which they both agree on. Certain things will be taken to be food, other places will be regarded as shelter, and each will start to assume particular daily chores. These habits for the two people can be easily changed by them (Berger & Luckmann, 1966, p. 58). Nevertheless, in later generations, these habits will be treated as rules to be followed. There will be definite roles for women and ways of building a house. Later, this will become the reality and absolute truths, where people in that generation will tend to believe that it is how the world runs (Berger & Luckmann, 1966, p. 60).

In relation to mental illness, absolute truth does not exist, but social constructions are the ones which make up the idea on the existences of mental illnesses. A human being is seen as an object which can be examined, given a diagnosis, and treated in a similar manner to a machine. Because of this belief, people affected by mental illness who live in a society where there is the view that absolute truth does not exist rarely seek treatment from mental health professionals.

Cognitive closure plays a major role on the stigma associated with mental illness because of the various stereotypes which are linked to the illness. The need for cognitive closure has contributed to the stigma which those affected by mental illness experience because of the stereotype attached to the mental illness. These stereotypes tend to group those affected by mental illness as people possessing negative traits or being the same (Corrigan, 1998). When a person seeks psychiatric or psychological help, the society perceives them as being insecure, sad, or unsociable (Sibicky & Dovidio, 1986).

An example of the need for cognitive closure is when a person dies among the aboriginal people, they see the person's spirit. In the Western culture, if a person claims to see or hear things that are not visible, they are diagnosed with psychosis. This is a case of the need for cognitive closure. In this case, the Western culture stigmatises the aboriginal people because of ignorance they have in regard to the culture of the aborigines since the Western people feel the need to get answers on everything.

People affected by mental illness are usually described in a vague manner. An example is when the person is referred to as being violent or dangerous. By doing this, the public continues with the generalisations which are adverse (Corrigan & Watson, 2002). Cognitive closure relies on assumptions and stereotypes towards people affected by mental illness. These stereotypes tend to make the public distance themselves socially from people affected by mental illness (Angermeyer & Dietrich, 2006). A person who portrays violence and is irrational and unpredictable is termed as being affected by mental illness since the people around the them feel the need to get an answer on the person's behaviour. Because of the stigma which comes from the stereotypes related to mental illness, those affected tend to conceal the illness to avoid the stigma.

Cognitive closure brings with it another stereotype, where if a person is labelled as being mentally ill, they are regarded as being dangerous, and people tend to avoid the person since the need for cognitive closure makes the public feel they need to interpret the person's behaviour. Those affected by mental illness are perceived as being different from the rest of the society. This determines the kind of treatment they receive from those around them.

An example is where a crime which is violent has been committed and two people are suspected to have committed the crime. One person is affected by mental illness, while the other one is not. Because of the stigma associated with mental illness, and the person affected by mental illness is viewed as dangerous and violent, there is a high likelihood that this person may be given a verdict of being guilty in comparison to the person who is not mentally sick. The jury feels the need to conclude that since people affected by mental illness are 'dangerous and violent', then the one who most likely committed the crime is the one affected by mental illness.

When someone is arrested and they have severe mental illness, the individual is given a stiff sentence because of the existing stereotype stating that the person is dangerous (Tellier & Felizardo, 2011). The need for closure where those people affected by mental illness are regarded as being violent influences the jury's decision. When a person is labelled as being mentally ill, rarely will any employer want to hire the individual. Also, landlords may be unwilling to rent apartments to people affected by mental illness. These stereotypes make the individual fear interacting with other people (Link et al., 1989) since they are looked upon suspiciously.

The need for cognitive closure can lead to hindering the person affected by mental illness from accessing mental healthcare. The reason is, in some culture, mental illness is associated with evil spirits, and since this is the view of the family or society, the affected person may not be required to go for a treatment from a health professional. An example is in South Asia, where mental illnesses are linked to a demonic possession, the lack of faith, and the evil eye. This can deter the affected person from seeking mental healthcare from a medical professional (Amri & Bemak, 2012, p. 50).

The need for cognitive closure can also influence the treatment method which the person affected by mental illness, together with the family, prefers. For example, the people of Puerto Rico believe that sickness is caused by the fluids from a person's spirit and those of the dead who are close to the person. The method used to cure the person is prayer and purification. The individual is not taken to a mental health practitioner since the people in this society have a closed mind regarding the cause of the illness (Baez & Hernandez, 2001).

The need for cognitive closure in a society leads to social avoidance by the community for those affected by mental illness and their families including their caregivers (Angermeyer & Dietrich, 2006). The community may avoid the person because of having a closed mind where they the person affected by mental illness as being dangerous (Corrigan et al., 2001). In the Chinese culture the public avoids interacting with a person affected by mental illness, to the extent that no one would want any marriage relationship either with the affected person or their families.

Self-Medication due to Stigma Associated with Mental Illness

Self-medication is the behaviour where a person uses substances or drugs to administer treatment to themself without consulting a health professional (Castel et al., 1997). Over-the-counter drugs, which rarely require prescription from a health personnel, are most commonly used in self-medication. The person who is self-medicating uses the medicine without having discussed the symptoms with a health professional. People affected by various mental illness self-medicate because of the stigma which arises as a result of a person being diagnosed with mental illness or disorder. There are various drugs which are mostly used in self-medication. They include the following:

Stimulants - Methamphetamine and Cocaine

Stimulants intensify a person's pleasure by creating a spike in one of the brain's transmitters (dopamine) that sends messages to the person, telling them to be happy. These stimulants can also heighten the person's focus, attention, and energy, causing the person to be awake for long periods (Khantzian, 1987).

Alcohol

Alcohol communicates with the brain to help in reducing anxiety and inhibitions and increases the person's level of happiness. It helps in relieving stress. Since it is a depressant, it slows down the central nervous system's functions. Alcohol can alleviate tension temporarily (Drake & Wallach, 1989).

Marijuana

This substance has both a depressant and hallucinogenic effect. It helps in making the individual relax. Marijuana can also be used by people suffering from insomnia since it can induce sleep.

Depressants Drugs - Sedatives and Tranquillisers

These drugs are usually given as a prescription in treating various mental illnesses. A person may use them without proper prescription from a mental health practitioner. People affected by insomnia and anxiety can use them to help them in their sleep and be able to relax.

Opiates Which Include Heroin and Morphine

People affected by mental illness may abuse heroin since it helps in enhancing happiness and making dull feelings of stress and anxiety. This substance can also help in decreasing tension and elevating feelings of relaxation (Khantzian, 1987).

Reasons People Affected by Mental Illness Self-Medicate

There are different reasons people affected by mental illnesses and disorders may choose to self-medicate, and they include the following:

To Be Able to Cope with the Illness

Different mental disorders have different symptoms and modes of treatment. A person may self-medicate in order to control the symptoms or alleviate the side effects of the prescribed medications. For example, a person diagnosed with schizophrenia and is experiencing hallucinations may self-medicate in the hope that the hallucinations will cease. They may use alcohol, which may bring a false feeling of relief, but the delusions and hallucinations may become worse since the person is taking medication. Another example is a person affected by bipolar disorder using marijuana, cocaine, and alcohol in order to fight anxiety, insomnia, and shifting of moods which come with the disorder. The marijuana may be used to help in calming the person, while they may use stimulants to raise up their moods when in a depressive state.

Because of the side effects of the substances abused by the patient, their recovery process may be slowed down and become complicated since the withdrawal symptoms associated with the drugs may be similar to those of the disorder.

People affected by anxiety disorder may abuse alcohol in order to be able to relax and be calm. The person, because of the nature of the disorder, may not be able to enjoy leisure time with friends and family. By taking alcohol and illegal substances, they may get temporal relief (Bolton et al, 2006). The person may eventually become dependent on alcohol and substance abuse, necessitating the need for them to require treatment from substance and alcohol abuse.

Calming Some Particular Symptoms

Some people use self-medication as a way of calming or soothing some symptoms which they are aware of. For example, a person who is affected by social phobia and is unable to speak publicly or attend a crowded place may use some drugs to help them deal with the symptoms (Bolton et al., 2006). Though at the beginning, the person may get the desired result, that is, if they needed to go for an interview, the medication may help them be calm, but later, they become dependent on the drug.

Being Undiagnosed with Mental Illness

At times, a person may self-medicate since they are unaware of having any mental illness. For example, a person who has social anxiety may tend to believe they only drink to be able to enjoy themselves in a party or a social gathering. The person unknowingly is treating symptoms associated with anxiety disorder. The self-medication may become worse, which results in the person consuming more alcohol and other substances with an aim of controlling the anxiety.

Self-Medication due to Stigma Associated with Mental Illness

Mental illness brings with it stigma in many societies. To avoid the stigma, a person may opt to use drugs which are not prescribed by a mental health practitioner to control the symptoms and be accepted in the community (Corrigan, 2004). For example, an individual affected by social anxiety may choose to consume alcohol in order to deal with thoughts which hinder them from going to social gatherings. Another example is where a person affected by depression may take marijuana to numb the feelings of hopelessness and guilt. The substance may offer temporal relief but later lead to addiction and dependence on the substance.

To Help Deal with Discrimination Which Comes with Mental Illness

People affected by mental illnesses suffer from discrimination and various stereotypes. An example is where the person is labelled as violent and dangerous (Crisp et al., 2000). In order to deal with this prejudice, the person may self-medicate to numb the pain that comes with discrimination.

Culture

Culture plays a major role in how a community perceives a person affected by mental illness. In some cultures, such as in Asia, it is a taboo to talk about mental illness since it is associated with shame (Kishore et al., 2011). The people affected by mental illness in these communities may opt for self-medication in order to save their face in the community and avoid shame. There are other cultures which believe that mental illness is a result of evil spirits. The person, because of this belief, may look for relief for the symptoms which they may be experiencing through self-medication (Amri & Bemak, 2012, p. 50).

Denial

A person affected by mental illness may live in denial, not wanting to go to a mental health professional since they are afraid of the diagnosis. The person may choose self-medication rather than treatment in a psychiatric hospital.

Risks Associated with Self-Medication to the Mentally Ill Person

There are various risks that arise because of self-medication to the person affected by mental illness. They include the following:

Inaccurate Diagnosis

Self-medication can lead to wrong diagnosis, which can bring severe side effects on the person. A person ends up treating symptoms not related to the illness. The person can also think they have no illness, or they may think they are more ill than they actually are. For example, a person may think that they have a bipolar disorder because of experiencing mood swings. They may end up self-medicating, yet they could be having depression or borderline personality disorder, which exhibit the same symptoms.

Incorrect Dosage

Self-medication often leads to wrong dosage since the prescription is not from a qualified health professional. There is a risk of overdosing since the person does not know the right dosage to use. The person, rather than improving in their mental condition, may end up having addiction to the drugs which they are using to self-medicate.

Postponing Treatment

People affected by mental illness may delay their treatment through self-medication. The outcome may be dangerous since it can result to death. Also, by the time the person is seeking medication, the recovery process may take long since the illness has advanced in level, and managing or controlling it becomes difficult.

Addiction

A person abusing alcohol to control symptoms related to mental illness may start with only a few bottles. In a bid to control symptoms which may be on the increase because of the consumption of alcohol, the individual ends up increasing their consumption of alcohol. Eventually, the person becomes alcohol dependent. This applies to all other substances, such as cocaine, marijuana, and over-the-counter drugs.

Dual/Comorbid Diagnosis

Substance abuse while a person is taking medication related to mental illness is referred to as having a condition which is co-occurring and may require dual diagnosis (Drake et al., 1991). This makes it difficult for the mental health professional to be able to identify whether the symptoms the person is experiencing are related to drug abuse or medication for the illness. Though treatment is available, it takes an extended period, and the recovery process is slow.

Less Likelihood of Seeking Medical Treatment

The more a person self-medicates themself, the less likely they are to seek for help from a mental health professional. This eventually worsens their condition.

Ways of Overcoming Self-Medication as a Result of Mental Illness

There are various steps or treatment methods which a person affected by mental illness and is self-medicating can take to stop the addiction or dependence on the drugs. There is no particular treatment which works for all patients who have dual diagnosis. A person affected by mental illness who is under medication and is using various illegal substances, such as cocaine and marijuana among others, is said to be having co-occurring disorder or a dual diagnosis. The person needs treatment. There are various ways to treat the person; they include the following:

Inpatient and Outpatient Rehabilitation

The person needs first to recognise that they need help. The family can help in identifying a rehabilitation centre where the individual can receive admission. In the centre, the person receives mental and medical healthcare throughout the period they are in the rehabilitation centre. Most rehabilitation centres offer both the treatment for the addiction and for the mental illness or disorder. While in the residential rehabilitation centre, the person learns new skills on how to cope with the illness. In most cases, the person may be having a low self-esteem. During the rehabilitation process, the person builds on their self-esteem and self-worth (Torrey et al., 2000).

The inpatient rehabilitation centres are suitable for treating patients having a dual diagnosis since there is more time where the patient is able to gain trust with the mental health professionals. The treatment for both substances abuse and mental illness are done in a single setting, such that the patient is able to focus solely on the rehabilitation. For patients who may be in denial regarding their condition, they are able to get encouragement which helps them in accepting their condition and looking for ways to recover. The peer support in the residential rehabilitation centres helps since the patients are able to encourage, give hope, and advise one another.

There are also programmes for patients who require little supervision in the recovery process; these are the outpatient rehabilitation programmes. The programmes can be conducted in rehabilitation centres, mental health facilities, and clinics in the society. The patients receive the treatment during the day or in the evening but later goes back home. When comparing the inpatient and outpatient rehabilitation programmes, the outpatient programmes is less effective since the patient would require to be highly motivated to comply with the programme. In most circumstances, few patients affected by mental illness are able to comply with the routine.

Support from Family and Friends

An individual who has a co-occurring disorder needs support from their family, caregivers, and friends. The people around the person need to educate themselves concerning addiction and the mental illness which has affected the individual. Boundaries should be set where the person has limited access to the drugs. Where children are involved, the person should not bring the drugs to the house. The person affected by the dual diagnosis should be encouraged to look for mental health treatment, and during recovery, the family and friends should be supportive. This will aid in faster recovery. Support groups are also essential during the person's recovery process (Stroul, 1989). The group offers the individual encouragement since they are able to freely share their challenges and successes.

Psychotherapy

Therapy is a useful tool in the treatment of co-occurring disorders. It can be done at a personal or group level. An example of an effective therapy is the cognitive behavioural therapy. This therapy is useful in treating both mental illness and addictions. The therapy aims at assisting the patient to learn new ways on how to live and unlearn the wrong notions which they have concerning their lives. The therapy bases its theory on the fact that a person's actions and behaviours are influenced by the perception they have regarding the world around them. When a person believes that they are of no value, they tend to behave in a manner which is not healthy since they feel they do not matter. The therapy is not just for the patient to only talk with the therapist; rather, it assists the patient to set and achieve goals for their lives. The person learns to ask themself critical questions. For example, a person affected by an obsessive-compulsive disorder may ask themself whether doing the rituals can protect their family against harm or if they are only acting impulsively without logical thoughts.

There are other kinds of therapies where the patient is taught on techniques to use for relaxation. These techniques involve yoga, breathing, and meditation exercises among others. The techniques which should be taught by instructors who are trained are effective in treating depression, anxiety, and pain. For example, a person experiencing anxiety may self-medicate in order to relax, but if they learn relaxation techniques, the desire for the substance or drug which makes them relax and is addictive may wane with time.

Family Therapy

It is important to include the family of the patient with the co-occurring disorder during the treatment and recovery process (Stroul, 1989). The patient's addiction may have caused damage in the family. The damage could be emotional, financial, or relational. During therapy, the family will be able to heal and learn better ways on how to communicate with the person.

Support after Treatment

In order to ensure that the patient does not have a relapse, the therapist and the client should have an aftercare plan, whose aim is to address an ongoing basis the treatment needs of the patient. The patient should also ensure that they have mental healthcare continuously. This is to enable that the patient's recovery is sustained.

CHAPTER 4

Early Intervention And Stigma In Relation To Mental Illness

Fear of rejection and culture has been discussed at length in chapter 3 as one of the hindrances to seeking early intervention for people affected by mental illnesses. In chapter 4, obstacles that hinder early intervention will be discussed in detail and on ways in which a person can conquer them.

Early intervention in mental illness can be defined as the process where an individual who may be experiencing first signs of mental illness gets professional intervention and support. It can also mean detecting and treating mental illness at its early stages, especially for those people who could be experiencing their first psychotic episode (Commonwealth Department of Health and Aged Care, 2000). Early intervention can focus on either prevention or treatment.

Prevention is mostly for individuals who may be exhibiting their first symptoms of mental illness. The purpose is to avert the progression of the disease. The treatment focus is on those people who are already experiencing a mental illness episode. The treatment aims at reducing the period which the person affected by mental illness will take to recover and the adverse effects of the disease on the person's quality of life.

The delay in getting treatment for mental illness and disorders can slow down the recovery process. Early intervention assists in reducing the advancement of the disease and improving the physical and mental health of the person. The process should start with the unborn by checking the mother and, later, the children who seem to be at risk of getting mental illness. A general health practitioner can examine the child, and when the need arises, the child can be referred to a psychiatrist or any other mental health professional.

Early intervention and treatment helps in reducing the burden of mental illness on the affected person together with the family. The intervention can also reduce the chances of the person becoming disabled because of mental illness.

Reasons Stigma Hinders Early Intervention

People affected or exhibiting symptoms of mental illness may delay in seeking medical healthcare because of the fear of being branded as mentally ill. These people, together with their families, may be aware of the illness, but the shame which comes as a result of mental illness may hinder them from seeking treatment (Sirey et al., 2001). On the other hand, the fear of being stigmatised against can lead an individual to seek early intervention for the mental illness which can reduce the stigma (Filacovic et al., 2007). Many people affected by mental illness prefer to suffer in silence rather than seek medical intervention because of the stigma associated with mental illness.

A person affected by mental illness may fear the negative stereotype, where the society sees them as being responsible for the disease, leading them to ignore the symptoms which may indicate the presence of mental illness. Stigma can hinder a person from seeking early intervention to avoid discrimination from the public as a result of the mental illness. An example of bias is when some communities oppose policies which are geared towards increase or the provision of funds for mental healthcare (Olstead 2002).

In the Asian society, seeking help is a sign of weakness. To avoid the stigma of looking weak, the individual who is affected by mental illness may avoid seeking help early enough (Kishore et al., 2011). Those who are in employment may delay seeking early intervention for the mental illness to hide their status from their colleagues who, on knowing they have mental illness, may stigmatise against them (Bos et al., 2009).

Sometimes the fear of experiencing social distance from family and friends can deter a person from seeking early help for their mental health (Link et al., 1999). An example is where landlords become unwilling to rent out their house to the person who is branded as mentally ill (Corrigan & Penn, 1998). Another example is when employers are not ready to hire someone who is affected by mental illness (Stier & Hinshaw, 2007). To avoid this kind of stigma, the affected person may opt not to seek early treatment. Stigma from the society can bring with it low self-esteem and shame. All these can act as a hindrance in looking medical care early enough for those affected by mental illness.

There are some medications given to people who are affected by mental illness, whose side effects are physically visible. For example, some medicines used for the treatment of schizophrenia can cause physical tremors. A person who has witnessed this in others, who are using this type of drugs, may avoid early treatment (Fenton et al., 1997). An individual can fear being judged wrongly by a mental health professional when they share with them the symptoms which they could be experiencing. To avoid this, the affected person can decide not to seek treatment early enough (Pirkis et al., 2001).

The age of an individual can also inhibit their desire to seek for early intervention for mental illness. The older people may not be as responsive to treatment because of the age factor as the younger generation (Gallo et al., 1999). The society may hold the opinion that when an older person takes away their life, it is not as devastating as when a young person does the same. Thus, taking away of life, which is a mental illness, is more prevalent in the older generation because of lack of early intervention. Depression can also be regarded as being acceptable among the older people as a result of the losses they could have encountered in their lives. This kind of stigma will prevent an older person with either suicidal thoughts or depression from seeking early treatment or intervention.

In psychiatric or medical facilities, the older individuals, at times, do not receive adequate treatment. This can lead them to seeing no need of seeking early intervention for mental illness (Katon et al., 1992). The mental health practitioners mostly opt to give medication which, at times, have severe side effects, rather than therapy to the older people (Kaplan et al., 1999).

Ethnic minorities at times receive secondary healthcare because of racial prejudice, which prevents many of them from seeking treatment early enough for their mental condition. The young people seeking treatment for mental illness, at times, are turned away by the mental health professionals who regard the young people's symptoms as not being severe. The healthcare personnel may also be unequipped in dealing with mental illnesses; this may prevent many people from seeking early treatment for fear of being misunderstood by the healthcare professionals.

Ways of Encouraging Early Intervention for Those Affected by Mental Illness

There are various ways or methods which can assist in encouraging those that are affected by mental illness or are at a risk of developing mental illness to seek early treatment from a mental healthcare facility. They may include the following:

Educating the Society on Mental Illness

When the society has the right information regarding mental illness, there is a reduction of stigma towards those affected by the disease. Those in the community who should be the target of the education are the family of the affected person, the caregivers, and the general population. The information should be culturally acceptable so that the community can embrace it. The objective of the education will be to enable the community, identify any person affected by mental illness among them, and encourage them to seek treatment.

Establishing Early Intervention Programmes for Children at Risk of Developing Mental Illness

Children born of parents who are affected by mental illness are at a higher risk of developing the disease later in their lives. To prevent this from occurring when the mother is pregnant with the child, she should be given the right kind of care and support to avoid passing the illness to the unborn child. There are some viral infections which can cause schizophrenia for the unborn children. Lack of the right nutrition for an expectant mother for the first six months can cause the foetus to develop schizophrenia, so early intervention is critical.

Establishing Mental Health Services for the Youth in the Society

Adolescence and youth is a time of change; it is in this period when young people are at a high risk of developing mental illnesses. The young people, in most instances, resist seeking medical intervention. Establishing mental health services which are attractive to the young people can encourage them to get an early intervention on matters about mental illness. The mental health services can include programmes on the impact of drug and substance abuse and how this relates to mental illness and suicidal behaviours. These health services can make use of stories and videos from other young people affected by the disease, the challenges they could be experiencing, and their recovery process (Keys, 1997). Since most young people are Internet savvy, this can become a significant tool in providing information on various mental illnesses, their symptoms, and the treatment methods available.

Expanding the Support Given to Families and Caregivers of the Affected Individual

Some mental illnesses are at a higher risk of relapse; this places an enormous burden on the families and caregivers of the affected person. The family should get support, especially those in the rural areas who may feel segregated from the rest of the society. Also, children whose parents are affected by mental illness would require support in accessing healthcare to avoid developing the disease. Australia has developed a programme which is the National Framework for Protecting Australia Children 2009–2020 to assist in protecting children whose parents are affected by mental illness against neglect and child abuse. Doing this will help in reducing the stigma which families who have one of their members affected by mental illness undergo. Also, many more families and caregivers will seek early intervention for those among them, displaying who are at a risk of developing mental illness.

Educating the Mental Health Professionals on How to Identify and Prevent Deaths through Suicide

As discussed earlier, older people exhibiting symptoms indicating that they may want to take away their lives are not taken seriously by the mental health professionals since having them take away their lives is seen as not being tragic in comparison to a young person who does the same (Gallo et al., 1999). The health professionals should get training on how to identify the symptoms which can lead to death through suicide and on the strategies to use to lessen the risk. Where there are groups of people, an example of those in incarceration who are at a higher risk of taking away their lives, the mental health professionals, with the help of the training, will be in a position to avert the situation.

Early intervention programmes should ensure that the affected person receives treatment in a manner which least restricts them. The client and their family should be involved in selecting the most suitable treatment setting for the person.

Instituting Programmes for the Increase of Employment Chances to Those Affected by Mental Illness

There need to be more programmes that give people affected by mental illnesses prospects of getting employment. Employers, together with their staffs, should receive training on mental illness symptoms and the kind of assistance to give to the affected person; this will assist in early intervention. Employment can aid in initial response; this is because a person may be among the co-workers who are caring who can detect first signs of mental illness. Employment boosts the person's self-esteem, reducing the symptoms related to the mental disease, thus increasing their sense of self-worth (Frost et al., 2002).

Benefits of Early Intervention

There are various benefits which arise as a result of early intervention of mental illness. They comprise the following:

Timely Provision of Treatment

Treatment provided on time reduces the chances of a relapse and increases faster recovery. An example is when the bipolar disorder is detected early; there is a reduction in its severity, and there is an acceleration on the patient's response to the treatment. Early intervention and treatment can also aid in preventing the occurrence of other mental illnesses, such as schizophrenia. The recovery process takes a shorter period when early intervention is involved.

Reduction in the Need for Hospitalisation

Delay in getting treatment for any mental illness, at times, can lead to hospitalisation as the treatment becomes extensive. Admission can have adverse effects on the person and their family because of the financial burden and the time that the process will consume. The individual can also lose their identity and think themself only as patients (Wittman & Keshavan, 2007). Early intervention can result in the person affected by mental illness receiving treatment at their homes, which can assist in faster recovery as the person is surrounded by the people they are familiar with and make them comfortable during the treatment and recovery process.

Less Family Distress and Disruption

Mental illness brings with it a lot of stigma from the society; an example is in China where families of people affected by mental illness are regarded as being socially polluted (Rao et al., 2014, p. 287). This stigma can result in family members blaming the person who is affected by the illness; early intervention can assist the family to evade this kind of stigma. The rehabilitation process can also take a toll on both the patient and their family regarding finances and the time they have to take care of the patient during rehabilitation. This, too, can be avoided by intervening early.

Lower Rates of Deaths as a Result of People Taking Away Their Lives

People affected by mental illness are at a higher risk of taking away their lives in comparison to those people who do not have any mental illness. An example is in the case of bipolar disorder where psychotic symptoms, such as hallucinations and delusions, if left untreated, can result in death through suicide. Many mental illnesses can cause a person to behave differently from the rest of the society. This attracts public stigma, whose result can be the person taking away their life. Intervening early will reduce the risk of deaths where one takes away their life among individuals who are affected by mental illness.

Increase of Life Expectancy of Those Affected by Mental Illness

People affected by mental sickness suffer exclusion from health services. This can cause early deaths; for example, those affected by schizophrenia or bipolar disorder die younger than the general population. The premature deaths come since the person is normally at a higher risk of developing hypertension, diabetes, obesity, heart ailments, and cancer in comparison to the general population (DRC, 2006). Early intervention will thus reduce early deaths for those affected by mental illnesses.

Improvement of the Chances of Attaining Education

Mental illness can bring about the discontinuation of an individual's education. Early episodes of psychosis can hinder the affected person from attaining education (Kessler et al., 1995). Most mental illnesses and disorders cause the impairment of the cognitive, social, and emotional level of the person, such that, if they are students, they may become unable to continue with their education. Leaving school, without having any qualification, may obstruct or prevent the person from getting any gainful employment later in life, making them dependent on other people, which further increases the stigma that the person faces. Early intervention on mental illness can assist the person to complete their education, which will translate in their financial independence later in their lives.

Minimisation of Substance Abuse

People affected by mental illness may abuse various substances. An example is the use of heroin, which is a substance that temporarily enhances happiness, making dull feelings of stress and anxiety, reduces tension, and elevates feelings of relaxation (Khantzian, 1987). The abuse of drugs tends to worsen the mental illness or disorder as the person using them becomes dependent on them to function normally. The resultant issue is the co-occurring disorder, which can take an extended period for the person to recover. Early intervention will minimise the abuse of various substances and drugs as the symptoms of mental illness will be treated early enough.

Reduction in the High Cost of Absenteeism from Work

Mental illness requires the affected individual to get treatment from a mental health facility; this involves time. For those who are in employment, it may entail them being absent from work. This absence translates to costs which the business incurs because of the lost time and productivity. The employee receives their payment, even though they were absent from work, further translating to more costs incurred by the organisation due to absenteeism as a result of mental illness. Early intervention will help the business to cut down on these expenses which are related to absenteeism as the mental illness becomes treatable within a short period and the employee resumes back to work. In cases where the business or organisation waits for an extended period before an employee receives treatment for mental illness, it will take more time for the employee to recover and resume their duties.

Enhancement of Social Inclusion

An individual affected by mental illness suffers social stigma, where the person experiences discrimination from the society. According to Overton and Medina (2008), landlords rarely rent out their houses to a person affected by mental illness. Most employers are also unwilling to hire a person affected by mental illness. This kind of treatment from the public results in the person isolating themselves socially. Early intervention will reduce this type of stigma as the symptoms of mental illness will become manageable and the person can productively run their lives.

Immigrant Families and Mental Illness

Immigrant families refer to people who leave their home countries and go to settle in different countries. Immigrants encounter unique challenges about migration, which can cause mental illness. One of these difficulties or stressors which can contribute to mental illness among the immigrants in different countries comprises the trauma these people may have faced because of war in their countries. Also, some of the immigrants may have been living in refugee camps, which can cause trauma resulting in mental illness. Settlement in a new place, isolation, lack of employment, racism, and poverty are other challenges unique to immigrants that can trigger the occurrence of mental illness.

Other challenges which the immigrants encounter are culture shock in the new country, racism, language barriers, and discrimination, which can also cause mental illnesses among them. An example of how language barriers can cause mental illness is when an immigrant who cannot speak either English or French, which are the common languages in Canada, migrates there and experiences isolation, which can easily translate into depression or substance abuse. Experiencing discrimination can worsen mental illness as the immigrant who is affected, because of fear of stigma and discrimination, delays in seeking mental healthcare.

Examples of some immigrants and how stigma prevents them from seeking treatment for the early symptoms of mental illness are discussed below.

Asian American Immigrants

The Asian Americans comprise people from Southeast Asia, the Far East, India, and other Asian countries who have migrated to America. The Asian Americans, because of their cultural background, are inclined to hide early symptoms of mental illness as the disease is considered something which can bring shame to the family. Mental illness is a taboo topic among the Asian communities. Thus, it becomes difficult to disclose that a person or a member of their family is affected by mental illness (Kishore et al., 2011). Being socially segregated is a significant factor which contributes to the hiding of early symptoms of mental illness as the person, by revealing their status, may end up becoming a social outcast. An example is in China where the person affected by mental illness, together with their families, may lack someone whom to marry.

Asian Americans are less likely to look for mental healthcare, in comparison to the white Americans, to avoid the stigma associated with mental illness. Those affected by mental illness in the Asian community tend to be hidden from the public view, which further worsens the symptoms and makes treatment difficult. By not revealing the disease, the affected person is at risk of slowing down their recovery process when they later seek treatment. The Asian American community can also delay seeking treatment in a mental hospital because of fear of being misunderstood by the mental health professional as a result of the language barrier.

Since English is the second language for most people of the Asian origin, they tend to feel incapable of describing correctly the symptoms which they are experiencing as most words which describe mental illness among the Asians have negative insinuations. As these people do not want to be viewed as those who cannot speak the English language and face stigma, they usually opt to hide the illness.

People from the Asian culture are more likely to describe their somatic symptoms to a mental health practitioner but not the emotional symptoms which they could be experiencing to avoid being seen as weak (Lin & Cheung, 1999). In many of the Asian cultures, expressing one's emotion is seen as a sign of weakness, thus discouraging it in the society. An example is where a patient of the Asian descent may describe what they are experiencing in words, such as 'My stomach is hurting' or 'My heart is racing', rather than say what they are feeling by saying, 'I am feeling depressed.' Avoiding saying precisely what they feel helps them to avoid being stigmatised through putting on a display of strength.

The Asian Americans hold various myths about mental illness, which can prevent them from seeking treatment for early signs of mental illness. One of the myths held primarily by the immigrants from South Asia is that maintenance of strong family ties can help cure anxiety disorder, depression, and stress. When the affected person tries using the family ties as a source of their healing and it fails, they can become reluctant to seek medical intervention to avoid facing stigma from the community which may see them as having failed in maintaining strong family ties.

Another myth associated with mental illness among the Asian Americans is that by living a 'life which is good', where one meets the religious and family expectations, it is possible to avoid mental illness. When a person in this community discovers that they are having signs of mental illness, they may feel like they have failed in 'living the good life' expected of them by the society, thus becoming a shame to them (Amri & Bemak, 2012). This person may resort to hiding the symptoms to avoid tarnishing the family's name.

There is also the myth among the Asian Americans that mental illness can be treated through a person's will power. As weakness is not tolerated in this community, especially among the men, the person may end up hiding the mental illness, causing the condition to become worse over time and put at risk the individual's life (Kishore et al., 2011). The Asian culture also holds the belief that one should keep their problems to themself to avoid worrying their family and loved ones. This acts as a hindrance to seeking treatment for early signs of mental illness and disorders.

Lack of mental health practitioners who understand the beliefs and values of the patients can hinder people from the Asian American culture from seeking mental healthcare. A mental health professional needs to discuss the mode of diagnosis and treatment with both the patient and their family. When this is absent, the patient who is of the Asian origin may become reluctant to disclose their symptoms about mental illness to the physician.

Latino Americans

The Latinos are immigrants to America; they comprise people from Mexico, the Caribbean, and other countries from Central America. The majority of Latinos are natives, that is, they were born in America though a large percentage are immigrants. The beliefs and cultures of the Latinos who are immigrants can act as a hindrance to them seeking treatment for early signs of mental illness. These Latinos, in comparison to the whites, are less likely to regard mental illness as being medically abnormal (Romero, 2006). Only those people who exhibit violent and dangerous behaviours are taken for professional treatment. The immigrant Latinos believe in supernatural healing, which prevents them from seeking medical treatment when a person experiences early signs of mental illness (Luna, 2003). The most commonly found mental disease among the Latinos is depression (Aguilar, 2005).

Seeking medical help among the Latinos are seen as a sign of weakness and not the person viewed as being out of control. An immigrant Latino experiencing early symptoms of mental illness may delay or refuse to seek treatment from a mental health professional to avoid this kind of stigma. Many of the Latinos who are immigrants do not speak English but Spanish as their first language; thus, language barrier hinders many of them from seeking medical treatment because of the inability to communicate with the health professional (The Commonwealth Fund 2003). To avoid shame because of being unable to speak English, those experiencing signs of mental illness would prefer to hide their condition (Alicea, 2001).

The Latinos live as a close-knit society, where one can obtain help from family and friends. Having a close-knit society can prevent an individual from seeking treatment when they experience early signs of mental illness to avoid creating the image that they have left the society and family norms (Chiang et al., 2004). Most Latino Americans resort to family and friends for help on coping with life's issues, and one not wanting to be viewed as having deviated from is acceptable. The Latino Americans are religious and often seek spiritual help when they experience signs of mental illness, rather than professional treatment, to avoid the stigma of being regarded as different (Altarriba & Bauer, 1998).

A man among the Latinos is expected to be strong. By seeking medical help, they may appear to be weak. To avoid the stigma of being regarded as vulnerable, few men exhibiting symptoms of mental illness will look for mental healthcare in comparison to women (Kuo et al., 2006).

Muslim Immigrants in America

Another group of immigrants that will be discussed in this chapter are the Muslim immigrants who consist of Muslims born in a different country and have migrated to America or the children of these immigrants. According to CAIR (2010), there are an estimated seven million Muslims who live in America whose origin is an estimate of eighty countries from around the world (CAIR, 2006). A large group of these immigrants come from North Africa and the Middle East, though there are others whose origin is South Asia, Africa, Europe, and Central and South America (Pew Research Center, 2007; 2011).

The Muslims migrate to America in search of better employment and economic opportunities and to escape from civil conflicts in their countries. Similar to other communities, mental illness among the Muslim immigrants attracts stigma. Mental illness is imputed to the possession by evil spirits, lack of faith, evil eye, and bad karma (Aloud & Arthur, 2009). This belief can prevent an individual affected by mental illness or their family from seeking mental healthcare to avoid putting shame on their family as people who have no faith or are possessed by evil spirits.

The Islamic religion is viewed as a source of strength and healing, mainly about mental health (Ale et al., 2010). When a person develops mental illness, they are seen as people who have no faith in God (Erickson et al., 2007). Rather than to be regarded as having no faith in God, an individual would prefer to hide early signs of mental illness. To protect the family from shame and adverse opinion from the society, most Muslim immigrants opt to look for assistance from within their families and not from a mental health professional (Carolan et al., 2000).

Muslim immigrants, because of their cultural background, expect men to be strong, and in the circumstance where a man exhibits signs of mental illness, those around them encourage them to be strong and deal with the symptoms (Vogel et al., 2007). The man may delay in seeking treatment to avoid being branded weak. Most minority groups in the United States have experienced discrimination, oppression, and racism; Muslim immigrants are not an exception. Because of these factors, these immigrants may not seek help on any health-related issue, including mental illness, because of cultural mistrust (Chung & Bemak, 2012).

Muslim immigrants may feel that mental health professionals who are non-Muslim or who are American, because of the cultural barrier, cannot understand them, which further hinders them from seeking treatment early enough.

Immigrants in Canada

Immigrants in Canada account to one-fifth or 20 per cent of the Canadian population; they come from various places around the world, which include, Asia, South and Central America, and Africa (Canada's Ethnocultural Mosaic, 2006). They include those who migrated to Canada and those who have lived there for different periods as refugees. For some people, the process of immigration can be stressful and can become a contributing factor to the mental illness for the immigrants (Levitt et al., 2005). There can be an extended period before an immigrant gets citizenship in the country of migration. During this time, the immigrant may be leaving in harsh conditions. This may result in mental illnesses, such as depression and anxiety (Porter & Haslam, 2005).

At times, immigrants encounter hardships in finding work which is commensurate with their qualifications, and this can trigger mental illness (Beiser, 1999). Adapting to a new environment can bring emotional strain to an individual, affecting their mental health negatively. Immigrants in comparison to those who are natives of Canada, rarely seek treatment for mental illness (Chen, 2005). One of the reasons for the delay of the treatment for mental illness includes the inability to take time off from work for those who are employed. Also, language is a significant barrier for immigrants in Canada. In accessing medical care, there is the fear that the mental health practitioner may not understand their problem because of the language barrier. Some of the immigrants come from cultures where mental illness attracts stigma. Thus, a person exhibiting signs of mental illness may hide their symptoms to avoid stigma.

Some groups of immigrants often have to look for culturally acceptable ways to express the symptoms of mental illness. There is a high level of somatising signs of mental illness unconsciously to communicate them in a way which the person may not face stigma. Some of the ways of somatising the symptoms used are pain, vomiting, nausea, and shortness of breath. As these symptoms face less stigmatisation in comparison to symptoms of mental illness, the immigrant may hide the signs of mental illness, ending up not seeking treatment.

Some immigrants in Canada come from a culture where they hold the belief that mental illness can be overcome by one's self-will, thus not needing treatment. The outcome is that the affected person will hide early symptoms of the disease in a bid to overcome the symptoms through self-will. The immigrants in Canada also feel that the mental health services are not culturally sensitive, and these services fit only the natives of Canada. As a result, the immigrants experiencing early symptoms of mental illness may opt not to seek for mental health services. To avoid misdiagnosis or discrimination because of the incorrect stereotypes that the mental health practitioners hold towards the many immigrants' cultures, those exhibiting early symptoms of mental illness may avoid seeking treatment in mental hospitals.

Women who are immigrants in Canada may be unable to access mental healthcare because of their various responsibilities and roles in the workplace and at home. Women may even fear to lose their children after being diagnosed with mental illness, leading them in hiding early symptoms of mental illness.

Breaking the Stigma of Mental Illness among the Immigrants

To encourage more immigrants who are affected by mental illness to seek mental healthcare, the country in which these people have migrated to should come up with strategies which will help them to achieve this. Some of the strategies can involve the following:

Breaking the Language Barrier

Language barriers have been an obstacle when the immigrants are seeking treatment from the mental health professionals. Immigrants who are proficient in the English language seek for mental health services as opposed to those who are not proficient in the language. For example, since many of the Latinos who are immigrants are fluent in the Spanish language but not the English language, which is mostly used in America, they rarely seek treatment for mental illness from a healthcare professional (The Commonwealth Fund, 2003). To remove this obstacle, more professionals from the specific immigrant community should get training on mental healthcare; this will give confidence to more immigrants while seeking treatment for the mental illness. In places where there are no mental health professionals from the particular community, the use of professional interpreters can be made to make the immigrant comfortable during treatment. In the absence of a local interpreter, a telephone interpreter may be used (Lewis et al., 2005). The use of a professional interpreter is better in comparison with ad hoc interpreters, who may include friends, family, and staff in the health facility, as they assist in improving communication considerably (Flores, 2005).

Providing Mental Health Education

Some immigrants come from communities or countries where mental healthcare or treatment is offered to people whose mental illness is severe; an example is the Muslim immigrants. School curriculum should incorporate mental-health literacy programmes, where the children of the immigrants, along other children, are taught on mental illness (Wei et al., 2013). These programmes will assist in improving the attitudes and knowledge which the children will have towards those affected by mental illness in their community and, in turn, will reduce the stigma that is associated with the disease.

Both the mass media and social media can be used as a tool for educating the immigrants on mental illness; one example is in Canada where there is a newsletter, *StigmaBusters*, that assists in positively portraying those affected by mental illness. The mental health professionals can use the media to educate the society, which includes the immigrants, on mental illness' causes, symptoms, and available treatment methods. By educating the public, those experiencing early symptoms of mental illness will be bold to seek for treatment. Also, those who may be unaware that the signs they are exhibiting are related to mental illness will have the necessary knowledge on the steps to take. Psychoeducation should be offered to the community with a purpose of assisting them on how to identify the early symptoms of mental illness and the treatment methods available.

Incorporating the Families

Among the Asian Americans, the family's consent is required by the mental health professional during the treatment of the person affected by mental illness. To eradicate the mistrust which exists between the mental health professionals and the immigrants, the physician should start by meeting the family before meeting the patient. The family members should feel as a part of the treatment process. In cases where the patient does not adhere to the treatment, family members should be involved to discuss other treatment ways (Lewis et al., 2005). The Chinese immigrant patients in America, when they receive mental health interventions that incorporate their culture, tend to be more responsive towards the treatment offered.

Among Muslim immigrants, it would be culturally wrong to match a female client with a male physician or counsellor. Also, the father's role is significant in determining what mode of treatment is suitable for their children. The purpose of including the family is for the mental health professional to understand the cultural views of the patient's family concerning the origin of the illness and their expectations regarding treatment. This will encourage those experiencing early signs of mental illness to seek for treatment on time.

In Canada, most immigrants come from cultures which include the family when making decisions. For the mental health practitioners in Canada to be successful in treating the immigrants, the family members should be a part of the treatment process. The family can accompany the affected person during their visits to the mental health facility. Though the Canadian laws recognise confidentiality for youths who are above fourteen years, for cultures which acknowledge the authority of parents over adolescents, the Canadian law should incorporate this culture.

Among the Chinese immigrants, family and friends play a significant role when one is looking for solutions to a problem. Help from friends and family is most preferred among the Chinese; the health practitioner should thus include the family during the treatment process. An example of how Chinese people turn to friends for assistance is for Chinese immigrants who had tried to take away their lives, the support of the family was critical in leading them to seek for help (Chung, 2010).

Establishing Services That Are Community-Based

Most immigrants tend to seek for mental health services in facilities or hospitals which are not intimidating. Religious and community leaders can be included in forming mental health interventions suitable for the different immigrants. An example is where a patient is taught English while learning about mental illness at the same time; this will help more immigrants displaying signs of mental illness to seek treatment. Also, among the Muslim immigrants, there is a need to solicit the contribution of their religious leaders regarding the kind of medical intervention that is culturally acceptable to them (Reitmanova & Gustafson, 2008).

Among the Asian American immigrants, there are organisations within the community which hold mental health camps and public workshops where open discussions on mental illnesses are held. By incorporating mental health practitioners who have similar cultural backgrounds with the attendants of the workshop, the public becomes more receptive to the information being given. In case the physician cannot speak the local dialect, a speaker who is a native can help during the discussions. During the open forums, immigrants who have earlier on been diagnosed with mental illness and sought medical treatment can share their experiences. By sharing in their recovery process, immigrants affected by mental illness will be encouraged to seek treatment since the stigma associated with mental illness will be decreased.

An example of community-based services which have assisted in decreasing the stigma associated with mental illness is a twelve-week group forum offered to Latino American women. The focus was on women affected by depression (Valdez et al., 2013). Also, there should be the establishment of social-support systems given to immigrants to help them cope with changes that come as a result of immigration. These social systems will impact on how immigrants view mental health services and can encourage those with early symptoms of mental illness to seek treatment (Lorenzo et al., 2012).

Integrating Traditional and Modern Treatment Practices

The Western methods of treating mental illness should be sensitive to the culture of the immigrants. Among the Muslim immigrants, because of their cultural and religious views, they are more inclined to look for a cure in the Islamic religion (Abu-Ras & Suarez, 2009). During the counselling of the person affected by mental illness, the mental health practitioner may need to include the traditional and religious healers to know what is acceptable to the patient and the family during treatment (Bemak et al., 2003).

The mental health professionals also need to learn the culture of their patients to offer the right treatment to them. Typically, during a mental health diagnosis, the same kind of questions are asked to all patients to establish their mental health. The questions may include some culturally sensitive topics, such as sexuality or taking away of one's life which is considered a taboo subject, among the Muslim immigrants. Because of this, the patient may be reluctant or unwilling to give their answers. To avoid this from happening, the interview or diagnosis should be conducted in a manner that is sensitive to the culture of the patient.

The Latinos believe in conducting prayers and having personal and house purifications as forms of treatment for the person affected by mental illness (Baez & Hernandez, 2001). The mental health professionals working among the Latino immigrants can allow them to offer prayers as long as it does not harm the patient. The Latinos are religious; most of them, when they experience symptoms of mental illness, seek help from religious leaders. Thus, mental health services among the Latino immigrants should include the aspect of religion (Chaumba, 2011).

By incorporating the culture of the immigrants, it will encourage more people who may experience early symptoms of mental illness to seek treatment from a mental health facility as they feel that the health practitioners are not discriminating against them.

Using Technology

There are various interventions which are technology-based that can assist in removing the language barrier between the immigrants and the natives of the countries where they have migrated. Mental health professionals can offer online consultations to immigrants who are affected by depression. Through the use of video conferencing, the psychiatrist can talk with the patient who may experience early symptoms of depression, which can improve the quality of their lives (Moreno et al., 2012). Technology can assist the mental health professional in getting a comprehensive and well-grounded mental health examination of immigrants who may be unable or unwilling to go to mental health facilities.

Providing Mental Health Services in a Culturally Friendly Environment

Immigrants experience discrimination in various spheres of their lives from the natives of the countries which they have migrated to; this brings mistrust between the immigrants and the residents. The distrust causes the immigrants not to seek for mental health services, even when the need arises. An example is the Muslim immigrants in the United States of America who may become hesitant to seek treatment from psychiatric hospitals which looks threatening and uninviting to them. When the mental health services are offered in an environment or a place where they feel comfortable, such as the mosques, those displaying signs of mental illness can comfortably access these services since there will be no stigma attached to the disease. The idea behind this is to take the mental health services to where the immigrants are and not to wait for them to seek for treatments in the psychiatric hospitals, which at times, can have a disastrous effect on their mental health because of late treatment.

Consolidating Physical and Mental Healthcare

The treatment for the physical and mental illness are divided; because of this, immigrants affected by mental illness usually prefer to somatise the symptoms to access physical healthcare, which holds little stigma in the society. The integration of physical and mental healthcare can encourage many immigrants to seek treatment for physical symptoms and, in the process, receive treatment for mental illness. The Asian American immigrants have recorded lower rates of symptoms of depression as a result of the integration (Kwong et al., 2013). Latino American women who had suffered trauma preferred therapy from a mental health professional that is offered in a primary care facility (Ratzliff et al., 2013).

Breaking the Silence on Mental Illness

Among the Asian American immigrants, mental illness is a taboo subject, providing platforms where people who have been affected by mental illness and those who have recovered share their experiences publicly can reduce the stigma attached to mental illness. Doing this can encourage those experiencing symptoms related to mental illness to seek treatment from mental health professionals. The media can assist in reducing the stigma by inviting people who have recovered from mental illness to share the challenges they have encountered on their way to recovery. Also, they can share the available treatment methods and how the society needs to interact with a person affected by mental illness.

Media and Early Intervention of Mental Illness

In chapter 2, the role that the media plays in either promoting or decreasing the stigma associated with mental illness was discussed at length. This section will analyse how the wrong misrepresentation by the media on mental illness hinders those affected from seeking early treatment or interventions. Media is a tool which can control the mind and attitudes of the masses (Haley & Malcol, 1987). The media, through its wrong portrayal of mental illness, has caused an increase in mental illness as people are afraid to seek mental health services because of the stigma associated with the disease.

There are myths which the media portrays to the public regarding mental illness. These myths were discussed in chapter 2 and include people affected by mental illness being violent, unpredictable, and dangerous. Another common myth is that one cannot recover from mental illness. Also, the media holds the myth that adolescents who are affected by mental illness are only going through a phase. These beliefs or myths have contributed to a large extent in preventing those exhibiting signs of mental illness from seeking early treatment. The kind of media that is of interest in this discussion is the electronic media which consists of television, films, and radio. The media also includes the print media, which comprises magazines and newspapers, and the internet, and what harm they cause regarding mental illness.

Television and Films

Television is one of the most popular and extensively used sources of media. According to the research conducted by Nielsen Media Research in 2012, the minimum time an individual spent on watching television on a monthly basis was six days and fifty-four minutes (Holmes, 2006). According to Fox (2012), more people own television sets than a cell phone, which shows the extent to which television, through images and messages, can influence the public. Exposure to repetitive information shapes the society's perception concerning a particular subject (Gerbner et al., 2002, p. 49). Television, in most instances, gives information, which is harmful to the society's view on mental illness.

For most people, television is their primary source or reference concerning mental illness. These people rarely come into contact with those affected by mental illness. Most people rely on TV to provide them with information regarding the mental disease, which is erroneous (Stout et al., 2004). According to Philo et al. (1994), people can be described as consumers who are active; this means what they watch on television regarding mental illness adds to the information that they already have on mental illness. People who spend most of their time watching television usually end up having a cynical worldview regarding the mental disease because of the images and values which are portrayed on television (Gerbner et al., 2002, p. 47).

Television is hence a significant tool that influences the views which both those affected by mental illness and the public hold towards the disease. When television depicts mental illness in a way that is both scary and erroneous to the public and the general population, the people affected tend to suffer an increased level of stigma, leading to avoidance of treatment. There are times during prime-time news when television uses cases of violence and link them to mental illness as part of their headlines to get the attention of the public; this further strengthens the stigma that those affected by mental illness face (Corrigan, 2004).

When television presenters are reporting on mental illness, the language used to describe those affected is mostly derogatory. Terms such as *psycho, basket case, lunatic* among others are used. These terms are demeaning to those affected and their families, which hinders early intervention as the affected person would prefer to hide their condition to avoid the negative labels. Programmes on television describe a person affected by mental illness through their disease and not their individuality or personality. In most of these programmes, those affected by mental illness are shown as people who add no value to the society and people who are unproductive (Hoffner & Cohen, 2012). To avoid being viewed as unproductive and of no value, the affected person tends to avoid treatment.

Most films and movies depict people affected by mental illness adversely. Most of the people who play the character of the person affected by mental illness are portrayed as being out of control, being dangerous, and having a criminal nature (Singorielli, 1989). This negative depiction of people affected by mental illness creates fear in both the public and the affected person towards mental illness. There are also films which portray those affected by mental illness as a risk to both the society and to themselves. In most crime dramas, the violent offender's character is usually played by an individual who is affected by mental illness. In comparison to what the society believed fifty years ago, these negative depiction of mental illness has strengthened more the belief that those affected by mental illness are dangerous (Sieff, 2003). To avoid being seen as violent, a person presenting symptoms of mental illness may fear to seek early intervention.

There are television shows and movies that paint the mental health professionals as inhuman and evil. They are portrayed as being more mentally affected in comparison to their patients. The people watching this kind of television shows end up in believing this as the reality (Stout et al., 2004). Television programmes have a gender bias, which favours females affected by mental illness; they are shown to be less violent in comparison to their male counterparts. Television programmes and shows rarely portray the fact that only a small percentage of people affected by mental illness commit crimes (Klin & Lemish, 2008)

There are movies which portray mental illness as something that positively influences an individual's life or something a person should aspire to get, which is erroneous. An example of a movie that does this is, 'The charismatic psychopath is everywhere,' where ladies affected by mental illness are depicted as charming. This misrepresentation can prevent a person showing signs of mental illness from seeking treatment since they look at the disease as adding value to their life.

Another movie that gives misleading information on mental illness is *Full House*, where one of the characters affected by an eating disorder gets over the condition in three days. This information is incorrect as in reality, overcoming the disorder can take an extended period or, at times, years. People who are experiencing early symptoms of mental illness may be unwilling to seek for treatment because of the wrong information which is given concerning mental illness and mental health professionals on the television shows and films. The delay in seeking treatment makes it difficult to treat and control the illness.

Television trains people on how to treat or interact with those affected by mental illness. As most of the television shows paint those affected by mental illness negatively, the public will end in treating them adversely. For example, people affected by schizophrenia are viewed as unpredictable. This prevents early intervention as the person may not want to suffer isolation as a result of the diagnosis showing them being unpredictable (Crisp et al., 2000). Mental illness is depicted as being strange in comparison to other physical ailments. To avoid being viewed as 'strange', people affected by mental illness will tend to avoid treatment. Few people are willing to interact with those affected by mental illness because of the misrepresentation of mental illness on television shows (Lyons & Ziviani, 1995).

Newspapers and Magazines

At times, newspapers report on issues related to mental illness, such as taking away of one's life and violence, as part of their headlines. An example is the *Washington Post* on 6 December 1999, whose headline was 'Escaped Killer from Mental Hospital Is Shot'. Just as in television, criminal activities are linked to mental illness in newspaper reporting (Wahl, 1996). Newspapers tend to portray those affected by mental illness as being a threat and a danger to the society; this encourages stereotypes that are negative towards mental illness (Allen & Nairn, 1997). Newspapers also portray the people affected by mental illness as those deserving pity. To avoid this attitude, those affected tend to hide the sickness (Goulden et al., 2011). Most articles on newspapers report erroneously on mental illness; an example is anorexia being reported as a condition of the young white females (Saguy & Gruys, 2010). Another example is where articles which report on schizophrenia portray the affected people as violent and dangerous (Goulden, 2011).

The language used to report on mental illness in many newspapers is demeaning. Those affected by the disease are described as victims or people who are suffering. Derogatory terms such as 'schizophrenic' are used to describe someone who is affected by schizophrenia. These derogatory terms can hinder those affected from seeking treatment. Newspaper articles, at times, report on the people who have tried to take away their lives in a glamorous manner. An example is when a person who tries to take away their life is unable to is reported to have a 'failed suicide attempt'. This suggests to the society that the act itself has value. This kind of reporting may encourage the person portraying symptoms of mental illness to take away their life to be seen as a hero rather than someone seeking treatment from a mental health facility.

Mental illnesses are often inaccurately reported in various articles in the newspapers; for example, people affected by schizophrenia are reported as having a split personality (Boke et al., 2007). Symptoms of postpartum depression are exaggerated, and the newspaper articles tend to emphasise on those women who carry out violent acts against their children as having postpartum depression (Holman, 2011). In magazines, people affected by the obsessive-compulsive disorder are portrayed as stalkers. This has an impact on the affected person who may not take the disorder seriously, thus not seeking treatment. Also, rather than facing legal actions, the society may assume that those who stalk others are affected by the obsessive-compulsive disorder.

Most of the newspapers reports on various mental illnesses and disorders provide limited information on the symptoms, available treatment methods, and the causes of the different mental illnesses (Wahl, 1995). When those affected read these articles, they may not seek treatment as the articles may indicate that the person does not have any mental illness (Corrigan, 2004). Newspapers giving negative publicity towards mental illness helps strengthen the negative stereotype which the public holds towards mental illness and those affected. A person affected by mental illness may accept what the society says about mental illness, thus seeing no need of seeking treatment, which makes their state or condition worse (Rosenfield, 1997).

As those affected by mental illness are portrayed negatively in newspaper articles and magazines, they may not see the need to look for employment because of the fear that they may not get the job (Corrigan et al., 2003). Rarely do newspapers and magazines give a positive report concerning people who have recovered from mental illness or are in the process of recovery. Most of the newspaper articles are on people affected by mental illness and who have carried out a violent act or crime. Newspapers and magazines rarely write educative or informative materials to help the public learn on ways in which they can prevent themselves from mental illness. By newspaper articles depicting people affected by mental illness as violent and dangerous, few people would want to associate with them (Thornton & Wahl, 1996). To avoid this kind of treatment, a person presenting symptoms indicating the presence of mental illness may avoid treatment, further worsening their condition.

Internet

The Internet is a new medium for conveying information to the public. It includes social media such as Facebook, Twitter, Instagram, among others. The presentation of mental illness through the internet is different from traditional media such as television, radio, newspapers, and magazines. It is an interactive medium used mostly by young people (Smith, 2013). Social media has used derogatory terms to describe those affected by mental illness. Some of the words used are 'feeling schizo', to mean that a person is experiencing symptoms related to schizophrenia. This term is misused, thus reducing the seriousness of schizophrenia.

The wrong use of words about mental illness such as 'schizo' may cause the public start viewing those people affected by schizophrenia as only being moody. As a result, the society may not sympathise with those affected by schizophrenia because of the wrong portrayal on social media platforms. Some social media users also term people affected by mental illness as 'retards', which is a derogatory term. The use of such a phrase makes the public view people affected by mental illness as being unintelligent. To avoid these kinds of derogatory terms, people experiencing symptoms of mental illness would prefer to hide their state.

People who post on various social media sites on their mental illness are at a high risk of cyberbullying, which may further worsen their condition. Cyberbullying is a combination of verbal and social bullying; it can involve emailing, texting, and using social media platforms, such as Facebook, Twitter, and WhatsApp. Rather than facing cyberbullying, the people experiencing early symptoms of mental illness may end up not seeking for treatment.

Ways in Which the Wrong Misrepresentation by the Media of Mental Illness Hinders Early Treatment

Media misrepresentation of mental illness creates both public and self-stigma, which hinders the affected person from seeking early treatment. The person may be afraid to seek treatment to avoid making their condition becoming known in the society as this may have adverse effects on different spheres of the person's life which include the following:

Relationships

Media portrays people affected by mental illness as being different from the rest of the society. For fear of rejection, a person experiencing symptoms of mental illness may fear seeking treatment to avoid their status being disclosed to family and friends (Overton & Medina, 2008). When their state becomes public, the person may suffer from lack of social relationships as the public and, at times, their families become unwilling to live in the same house or neighbourhood with them. The individual may suffer exclusion in participating in civic activities as a result of the wrong information given by media that people affected by mental illness are 'dangerous', 'foolish', and 'unpredictable'. An example is when a person affected by mental illness is not allowed to serve on juries (Rethink, 2010).

Because of the wrong depiction by the media that those affected by mental illness are dangerous, if they are in a marriage institution, they may experience divorce. One of the countries where this happens is China, where mental illness is a ground for divorce. To avoid this, the individual may not seek early treatment to prevent their partner from realising that they are affected by mental illness. A spouse who is not affected by mental illness can limit the interaction the one affected has with the children. This is another reason for preventing one from seeking early treatment. In some occasions, a parent who is affected by mental illness may be denied the opportunity to take care of their children. To stay away from this, the parent may be reluctant to seek mental health services (Corrigan et al., 2001).

Mental illness can result in the breakdown of the relationships with one's family, partners, and friends. For the affected person to ensure that the relationship remains intact, they may avoid treatment to avoid becoming a burden to those around them. In some occasions, children whose parents are affected by mental illness suffer from bullying at school and in the society. These parents may delay in seeking treatment to protect their children against bullying (SEU, 2004).

Employment

Media has increased the level of stigma which those affected by mental illness experience. As a result, those affected tend to lack employment opportunities. They may apply for jobs which they have the right qualifications for, but because of the illness, they fail to get it (Alexander & Link, 2000). The person displaying early signs of mental illness may not seek treatment in order not to be discriminated against regarding employment by having their condition become public. Some medications used by people affected by mental illness, for example, schizophrenia, can cause them to have tremors which are physically visible leading to ridicule in the workplace. To avoid this, they may not seek treatment.

The media portrays some mental disorders as something which a person can quickly 'snap out'. An example is when a person affected by the anxiety disorder or depression is given a series of steps to follow on social media to come out of the condition. When the person tries this and it fails, the society views them as unwilling or lazy, and it can ruin their chances of getting employment (Thornicroft, 2006). The person may not seek for treatment since they believe what the media misrepresentation concerning their illness says.

Some organisations, because of the negative media portrayal, may not employ an individual who is affected by mental illness since the person is viewed as one who cannot perform their duties. Also, since those affected by mental illness are depicted as unpredictable by the media, there are employers who feel they would experience loss of customers on hiring a person affected by mental illness. The media holds the myth that one cannot recover from mental illness, making those affected and those whose condition is known to lack employment.

Some mental illnesses make employers unwilling to hire an individual who is affected by the disease (Stier & Hinshaw, 2007). For example, for people affected by depression, having been portrayed by the media as being weak and lazy, only few employers are willing to hire them (Reavley & Jorm, 2011). At times, when the person is employed, they are paid less in comparison to their colleagues who are mentally healthy. To avoid discrimination and stigma in the workplace, the person affected by mental illness may not seek treatment, which worsens their conditions and extends the recovery period.

Education

Because of the misrepresentation by media on mental illness, schoolgoing children affected by mental illness may discontinue their education because of the fear of rejection from the other students. These children could be experiencing symptoms where they are unable to concentrate in school or handle noise and large crowds. Also, they may not be able to meet deadlines and cannot make new friends. The parent may opt to hide this child and not seek treatment to avoid them being bullied at school.

Media should refrain from the adverse representation of mental illness to change the public's view and allow those affected to be incorporated as part of the society. The reporting language used on television, radio, and newspapers should not be derogatory. When violent crimes are committed, those affected by mental illness should not be linked to them until the media does an in-depth investigation. The 'people-first language' should be used when reporting. This will help in avoiding terms such as 'schizophrenic people'. Media reporting should be conducted in adherence to the international and national code of conduct in various countries. All these will reduce the stigma associated with mental illness and encourage those exhibiting early signs of mental illness to seek treatment.

CHAPTER 5

Steps In Reducing The Stigma On Mental Illness

The stigma faced by people affected by mental illness has been a significant theme of this book. In chapter 2, stigma was defined, and the two types of stigma were analysed in depth. In chapter 3, examples were given of how different cultures stigmatise those affected by mental illness. In chapter 4, the impact of stigma on early intervention was looked into and the harm which the media causes by reinforcing the stigma of mental illness.

Though not an easy task, in chapter 5, we will look into the various steps which can be undertaken to reduce the stigma of mental illness. The people who are affected by mental illness need to feel like part of the society; they need not feel ashamed while talking about their challenges with mental illness. Some of the steps that can be undertaken to reduce the stigma of mental illness include education, having face-to-face contact, positive counselling, choosing words and attitudes carefully while talking about mental illness to name just a few.

Educating Others

Education is one of the steps that can be used to reduce the stigma which is associated with mental illness. Since lack of accurate information on mental illness in the past has resulted in an increase of stigma on those affected, provision of the right information will help dispense fears, misconceptions, and myths which the public associate with people affected by mental illness. As people fear what they do not understand, education can be a significant tool in reducing the stigma of mental illness. When the society is armed with facts regarding mental illness, the stigma of mental illness will decrease.

Those people in the society who know about mental illness should pass it to others. When family members, friends, co-workers, and the media give on information which is incorrect, the one with the accurate information should be ready to challenge this erroneous information. The public should be made aware of the negative impact which the stereotypes that they hold and negative words have on those who are affected by mental illness. There are various avenues in which education can be provided, which include doing educational campaigns and incorporating mental-health literacy programmes in the school curriculum and educating the public and the families affected by mental illness among others.

Educational Campaigns

There is the typically held view that those affected by mental illness commit violent crimes. Education can help counter this erroneous belief by providing statistics which show that the rates of homicide are the same between the general population and those who are affected by mental illness (Corrigan et al., 2012). Educating the society on mental illness assists in diminishing self-stigma to those affected and building their self-esteem as the society begins to accept them (Cook et al., 2014).

Educational campaigns can be conducted both at the national and at the local level. An example of one of the campaigns which have proved useful in reducing stigma on mental illness is 'In One Voice' campaign in Canada, which has been done through social media. As a result of this campaign, the level of social distance towards those affected by mental illness has reduced. Educational campaigns are more effective among the youths than in the adults (Borschman et al., 2014).

Media, which includes social media, can be a significant tool in conducting these campaigns. As social media is popular among the young people, informative materials on mental illness should be put on online platforms where they can access it (Birnbaum, 2014). Doing this will help educate the adolescents and the youths who often turn to the Internet to seek information. This will help reduce the stigma of mental illness in schools and colleges. The mental health professionals, who include psychiatrists, mental health nurses, psychologists among others, should put mental health information on social media, where it is easily accessible. More books should be written on mental illness, their causes, symptoms, and methods of treatment which are available.

Incorporating Mental Health Literacy Programmes in the Educational Programmes

Students who are affected by mental illness can suffer stigma at school because of issues related to their behaviours, such as being absent from school; this can result in the student being disciplined by the teachers rather than receiving support. Mental health education in schools and colleges can assist in reducing the stigma among the schoolgoing children and college students (Wei et al., 2013). These programmes will help improve the attitudes, knowledge, and behaviours that the students and schoolgoing children will have towards those who are affected by mental illness in the school.

The educational system should include children and young people who are affected by mental illness; this will help schoolgoing children and students to learn how to interact with them. The introduction of mental health literacy programmes will help them become more accepting to those affected by mental illness since the young people in schools are at an age where they are beginning to form values which they will carry the rest of their lives.

The curriculum should aim at dispensing some of the myths held; an example is 'Those affected by mental illness are dangerous and violent' (Goulden, 2011). Including statistics showing that the rate of violent crimes in the general public is similar to the one among people who are affected by mental illness can dispense this kind of myth (Corrigan et al., 2012). Counsellors within the school should get constant training or refresher courses to assist them in handling students who are affected by mental illness in the school. Schools and colleges can regularly invite mental health professionals to give educational talks on mental illness. This will assist in reducing the stigma associated with mental illness in schools.

In Australia, a mental health programme in secondary schools has been established, which is referred to as the Mind Matters. An objective of the programme is to promote early intervention for secondary school students in Australia. Also, the programme aims at developing the emotional and social skills of the students to help them handle life's problems. Where they are students who are affected by mental illness, the programme enables the school community to create a conducive environment where they can learn. These strategies have a result of reducing the stigma in the secondary schools in Australia. In reducing the stigma, documentary films can also disease as a tool of conveying accurate information in schools on mental illness.

Also, adolescents in school can be taught on mental illness through programmes such as In Our Own Voice programme, which was developed by the National Alliance on Mental Illness (NAMI). This programme facilitates contact between people who are affected by mental illness and other members of the public. Also, puppets can be used as an anti-stigma tool among the adolescents as the message conveyed through the puppets is that people affected by mental illness are not dangerous, shameful, or threatening to the society (Pitre et al., 2007).

In medical colleges, the students come into contact with a medical culture where the mental health professionals hold a negative and harmful attitude to those affected by mental illness (Thornicroft et al., 2010). The mental health professionals' pessimistic view could be a result of seeing patients having several relapses despite treatment, which can strengthen the belief that one cannot fully recover from mental illness (Jorm et al., 1999).

The medical students, upon graduation, can be prevented from passing on the negative attitude to those affected by mental illness by incorporating programmes into their curriculum to dispense this negative view. The programmes should include modification of attitude; also, the education offered in medical schools should consist of a contact-based approach, where the students come into face-to-face contact with people affected by mental illness in the psychiatric wards. Furthermore, the medical students and other health professionals and people involved in mental healthcare should be taught on existing laws that forbid discrimination.

Educating the Community

Community education does not need to be formal; it can involve having group discussions on mental illness. An example is a report given by the National Health Commission in Australia in 2013 on the informal debate termed as 'Can we talk about mental health and suicide?' The findings were the public has not yet understood what mental illness is and that stigma linked to mental illness is a hindrance for treatment to those affected. These kinds of findings can be helpful in planning which areas need to be covered during community training on mental illness. In addition, the Schizophrenia Fellowship of New South Wales is an organisation which have changed lives of people affected by mental illness and their caregivers. Today, this organisation is based in an old Gladesville psychiatric hospital in Sydney and counts more than 2,200 community mental health workers all around Sydney.

Also, community education can involve distributing educational materials on human rights and other issues in connection with mental illness. An example of community education that has changed the attitude of the society towards people affected by mental illness is the beyondblue campaign in Australia, whose focus was to raise awareness of depression. Those that have been exposed to this programme were able to recognise early signs of depression and encouraged those affected by the society to seek treatment (Jorm et al., 2005).

Educating the Family

When a person is affected by mental illness, it impacts on their family and friends, their finances, their emotions, and their social well-being. The family of the affected individual suffers from stigma. Thus, it is necessary to educate them on mental illness symptoms, causes, challenges, and available treatment methods. There are only a few programmes which can help family members and caregivers to be able to deal with the stigma connected to mental illness. Lack of the right kind of information can hinder a family in detecting symptoms of mental illness, which one of the family members could be exhibiting.

As most people affected by mental illness live with their families, there is a need for the mental health practitioners to educate the family on how to take care of their loved one. The family also need to be taught on learning new ways of communicating with the affected person and, moreover, the treatment methods which are available, the side effects of the medications being used, and the symptoms of a relapse. Since mental illness can cause stress in the family, it is essential for the caregiver to learn on how to take care of themselves.

In the United States, there is the National Alliance on Mental Illness (NAMI), which is an advocacy group that stands for families and people affected by mental illness. This advocacy group gives support to those affected by mental illness, together with their families, through the provision of psychoeducation. NAMI has various programmes, which include Family-to-Family programme, Peer-to-Peer programme, NAMI In Our Voice, and NAMI Basics. The family-to-family programme's target is the friends and family of the person affected by mental illness. The training is done by a family member of a person who has been diagnosed with a mental illness; this person is usually first trained by NAMI.

This programme trains family and friends on how to cope with the person affected by mental illness; communication skills are also taught. Advocacy services are also provided during the training, and the families are directed to areas where they can get support after the training. Through the NAMI Family-to-Family training, families have been equipped with ways of solving internal conflicts which arise as a consequence of having a person in the family who is affected by mental illness (Dixon & Lisa, 2011).

The other educational programme offered by this group is the NAMI Peer-to-Peer which targets adults who have been diagnosed with mental illness. These adults are taught on the symptoms of mental illness, coping mechanisms, ways to interact with a mental healthcare provider, and ways to reduce stress. Through this information, the affected adult can manage self-stigma since they learn how to accept themself. The information also helps the adult who is affected to train the society on mental illness, thus reducing public stigma.

The NAMI In Our Own Voice programme involves people affected by mental illness sharing their experiences. Initially, it was started for people affected by schizophrenia. The programme aims to raise awareness of mental illness by focusing on stigma and equipping those affected by mental illness. The programme educates not only those who are affected by mental illness but also other groups of people such as students and law enforcement agencies. The programme has been successful in reducing the stigma which is associated with mental illness for both the affected person and their families (Perlick et al., 2011).

There is also the NAMI Basics, a programme whose target is parents or caregivers who have adolescents or teenagers affected by mental illness. Though the families receive education on how to care for the loved one who is affected mentally, it does not fail to recognise the unique difficulties which arise in providing care for a child affected by mental illness. The information given in this forum is different from that given to adults living with mental illness or their families.

Thus, education is a significant tool in reducing the stigma associated with mental illness. The governments of different countries, therefore, should come up with programmes and initiatives which will help educate its citizens about mental illness.

Attitude and Behaviour

Attitude refers to the way one feels or thinks towards someone or something. Stigma about mental illness refers to the attitude or behaviour held against mental illness or those affected by it. People who are affected by mental illness experience a double challenge: the first is the illness itself; the second one is from the negative attitudes and stereotypes which the society holds towards mental illness. These negative attitudes and behaviours hinder those affected by mental illness from accessing opportunities that enable them to live a quality life. Negative and harmful attitudes towards those affected by mental illness are widespread in various communities (Crisp, 2001).

For a long time, mental illness has been regarded as a private matter and a moral failure of the one affected, rather than a matter which involves the society as a whole and a disease that requires treatment (Whitley & Henwood, 2014). This attitude has adversely impacted on people affected by mental illness, and it has caused them to experience stigma from co-workers, mental health professionals, families, and fellow students (Ebrahimi et al., 2013).

There are various negative attitudes which are held by the society towards mental illness which need to change. Some of these views are being mentally ill as a sign of weakness and having no hope of recovery once a person is affected by mental illness. Other negative attitudes include people affected by mental illness are unpredictable, mental illness and insanity are similar, communicating with a person who is affected by mental illness is difficult, and mental illness happens to people from particular cultures only.

These attitudes and behaviours need to be changed; we need to realise that those affected by mental illness are human beings like the rest of us. This will help in reducing the stigma attached to the disease. The society needs to avoid putting labels on those affected by mental illness; statements such as 'He is bipolar', or 'That man is schizophrenic' should be avoided, the reason being a person is a human being and not a diagnosis. The proper way of describing the person is to say, 'He is affected by mental illness.' The right attitude and behaviour can reduce the stigma which comes as a result of one being affected by mental illness; growing up, we acquire various preconceived ideas and ways of thinking, particularly about mental illness. The society needs to see a person affected by mental illness beyond the disease and see them as people with an identity and unique attributes. The focus should be on the person's strength and capabilities and not the illness.

Negative attitudes influence the social distance which the public keeps towards people affected by mental illness. People who believe that those affected by mental illness are inferior would not want to associate with them. In contrast, those who hold a positive attitude towards mental illness will comfortably interact with the affected individuals in the workplace or maintain a friendship with them. People affected by mental illness experience negative attitudes from their families, employers, co-workers, mental health practitioners, and the media. The whole society needs to adopt a positive attitude towards mental illness by viewing the disease like any other health problem or ailment.

Various approaches have been used in changing the society's attitude towards mental illness though more needs to be done. One of the strategies that have proved useful in changing people's attitude towards those affected by mental illness is having face-to-face or direct contact with the affected person. As a result of this, most of the people who interact directly with a person affected by mental illness develop more trust and less fear, which reduces the public stigma (Islam & Hewstone, 1993).

The more a person comes into contact with the affected person, the more their negative behaviour and attitude towards them changes (Overton & Medina, 2008). In schools and colleges, students who are affected by mental illness should be allowed and encouraged to interact with those who are mentally healthy to change the negative attitude and behaviour that fellow students may be having about them (Pinfold et al., 2003). The affected students can also create a chance to share their experiences and challenges. Moreover, media can become a tool for enhancing face-to-face contact with people affected by mental illness by interviewing them or by having a person who has recovered or is in the recovery process share their experiences in the media.

Furthermore, contact can be established indirectly through videos where the affected person shares their experiences. Social media can be helpful, where those affected shares their experiences through online videos. When the public sees this individual talking about their experience, it can result in higher levels of empathy and less stigmatisation as previously held views on mental illness are challenged. The family and friends of the affected person can also talk about their experiences in taking care of a person affected by mental illness as they also suffer from stigma, which is referred to as family stigma (Larson & Corrigan, 2008). Family stigma comes as a result of the negative attitudes held by the society towards mental illness, which is extended to the caregivers, friends, and family of the affected person.

There is evidence that contact can lead to a change in behaviour regarding the attitude a person has towards those who are affected by mental illness. An example is a study that has been conducted, showing more funds have given to NAMI after people have come into contact with those who are affected by mental illness (Corrigan et al., 2002). When the society comes into direct contact with members of the society who hold important positions and are affected by mental illness, their attitudes towards mental illness tend to improve.

Also, communicating or giving the right information concerning mental illness can help in promoting a positive attitude towards those who are affected. Advocacy groups and groups that empower patients can assist in conveying the correct information on mental illness, with the aim of promoting positive attitudes in the society towards mental illness. The mental health professionals can help in changing the position and behaviour of the society towards those affected by assisting the affected person to integrate into the community.

Employers need to change their behaviour and attitude towards those people who are affected by mental illness; they need to develop a culture which includes diversity and which acknowledges an individual's competence and not their disabilities. There should be no discrimination during recruitment, training, and career development and on the day-to-day working life of all employees. Managers need to get training on mental health to enable them to accommodate those among them who are affected by mental illness. This kind of training can help dissipate the negative attitudes and assumptions held in the workplace concerning those affected by mental illness. One of the attitudes in the workplace that promotes stigma include viewing those affected by mental illness as being incompetent or lazy (Research by Secker et al., 2001).

Moreover, by employing more people who are affected by mental illness, other people within the organisation will start to view them positively. Also, when a person qualified for a particular position applies for the job, they should be hired despite the fact that they may be affected by mental illness as long as the symptoms are being managed through treatment (Stier & Hinshaw, 2007). Doing this will encourage more people who are affected by mental illness to see the need to look for employment as the fear of not being hired will be absent (Corrigan et al., 2003).

In cases where the employee affected by mental illness needs to go for treatment, the manager should regularly contact the employee to know of their progress. And when the employee finally returns to work, the environment should be conducive and supportive. Both the manager and staff should avoid discriminating against these employees. The mental health professional should also encourage this person to return to work after their treatment (Rinaldi & Pekins, 2004). In the workplace, there should be open discussions on mental health to encourage people who are affected by mental illness or are taking care of a loved one with mental illness to share their experiences; this will greatly reduce the stigma associated with mental illness.

Those who may be exhibiting symptoms of mental illness in the workplace should be encouraged to seek treatment by the managers and leaders of the organisation. Employers need to be educated to eliminate the myths they hold concerning the abilities of the employees who are affected by mental illness. Also, employers need to be taught on how to handle employees affected by mental illness; this will reduce the stigma associated with the illness (Corrigan, 2013).

The media is a significant tool that can help shape the society's attitude towards mental illness through a positive portrayal of mental illness and the people affected. By having campaigns done on stigma reduction, documentary films, and educative programmes, the community can start looking at people affected by mental illness as productive members of the society. The media should replace television shows that depict people affected by mental illness as violent with shows and series that portray them positively. Doing this will reduce self-stigma and public stigma on mental illness.

When speaking to or about people affected by mental illness, one should choose their words carefully as it can have a negative impact on the affected people. When referring to people affected by mental illness, words such as 'psycho' and 'crazy' should be avoided. In case the affected person wants to talk about their disease, one should listen to them and not brush off what the person is saying. Also, being judgemental should be avoided when talking to the affected individual, and respect should be maintained when communicating with the person.

The media should adopt 'People First Language' when reporting on mental illness; words such as 'depressed people' or 'schizophrenic people' should be avoided. On social media, terms such as 'feeling schizo' should be shunned as they make the public to view mental illness, particularly schizophrenia, as only a mood which a person can easily overcome. As a result, the society may not sympathise with those affected by schizophrenia because of the wrong portrayal on social media platforms. Other social media users term people affected by mental illness as retards, which is a derogatory term. The use of such phrases reduces the intelligence of those affected by mental illness. Words such as 'lunatic', 'crazy', and 'mad' should not be used in describing someone affected by mental illness.

Mental health professionals should work together with the media to encourage positive depiction of people affected by mental illness. Early training of medical students on positive attitudes about people affected by mental illness will help in forming their attitudes towards these people later in their interactions with them.

The Queensland government began an initiative in 2011 referred to as Change Our Minds, with the aim of reducing stigma on mental illness. The initiative's focus was on showing the society how negative attitudes and behaviours impact on people affected by mental illness together with their families. Through the initiative, the public has learned how to relate positively with those affected by mental illness through accepting and including them in social activities (Queensland Government, 2011). This initiative has impacted positively in the society since by receiving the right information concerning mental illness, the level of stigma against those affected by mental illness has begun to decrease.

In the United States, an organisation referred to as the American Psychological Association (APA) has assisted in the provision of the correct information to the public on mental illness and mental healthcare. The aim has been the promotion of positive attitudes towards people affected by mental illness, and encouraging them to seek treatment (Buetler, 2007). This organisation has availed information online on mental illness and treatment methods which are available to those affected.

The change of attitudes in the society and on a personal level will assist in promoting positive attitudes and behaviours towards mental illness and on those who are affected. The change of attitude and behaviour will reduce the level of stigma in the society

Positive Counselling and Therapy

Counselling about mental illness means establishing an interpersonal partnership between a patient and a mental health professional, with the aim of assisting the affected individual in changing their behaviours to function more productively in life (Buetler, 2007). Counselling can be viewed as a talk therapy where the client talks with a trained counsellor about their feelings and challenges. This is done in an environment which provides confidentiality. People affected by mental illness should realise there is no shame in receiving therapy as both counselling and therapy are significant tools in reducing stigma against mental illness. Counselling on mental health includes talking about challenges and problems which the affected person is experiencing to a trained counsellor. The person who is affected by mental illness can be encouraged to seek to counsel if those around them show them that they are not to blame for the illness (Rosen, 2003).

Counselling should be approached positively, that is, it should be seen as a way of taking care of oneself, and it is not for people who are in trouble only. By showing the affected individual that seeking therapy is a sign of courage and not weakness, it can lead them in approaching the process positively (Corrigan, 2004). During the counselling session, the mental health professional should treat the client with respect and dignity and listen to what they have to say regarding their challenges with the illness. Counselling helps in reducing self-stigma since the affected person becomes empowered, begins to accept themselves, has their hope renewed, and is taught life skills to support them in living a quality life.

There are different therapies and counselling services for the various mental illnesses. The different types of therapies are cognitive behavioural therapy (CBT), creative therapies, cognitive analytical therapy (CAT), psychotherapy, family intervention or therapy, dialectical behaviour therapy (DBT), and counselling.

Family Intervention/Therapy

When an individual is affected by mental illness, the family is also affected since at times, while taking care of the person, they experience stress (Carers UK, 2014). To deal with the stress and burden of taking care of their loved one, they require the necessary skills and information. This is where family therapy comes in—to help families deal with challenges which one of them could be experiencing because of mental illness. Family therapy is conducted in some sessions where the therapist meets the family members of the affected person. The meetings are divided into components that include engaging, assessing, formulating, and informing early warning symptoms.

There are some mental illnesses and disorders which can be treated through family therapy to reduce the stigma associated with them. Some of these disorders include depression, schizophrenia, bipolar disorder among others. The family intervention or therapy helps patients affected by schizophrenia by reducing the symptoms and the number of times that the patient has to be hospitalised. The result has been a reduction in isolation and social distance that those affected by mental illness suffer.

This therapy assists families who are affected by mental illnesses, such as schizophrenia. This reduces the risk of relapse for the patients. Doing this also helps those who attend to take their medications consistently, leading to a higher quality of life. As the recovery of those affected is quicker, the stigma against them is reduced. Families who have children and adolescents who are affected by depression can benefit from family therapy as they will learn how to efficiently communicate with them which will reduce the stigma against them.

Cognitive Behavioural Therapy

Cognitive behavioural therapy helps the person who is affected by mental illness to change on how they think and behave since this is connected to how they feel. This therapy looks at how one's childhood experiences have affected their behaviour. The cognitive behavioural therapy targets particular symptoms and helps the patient on issues that involve their esteem and their functioning socially. The therapy also helps the client to understand how their thoughts about themself and the people around them affect their reactions to different situations. As the affected person can understand themself better, self-stigma is reduced since how the public perceives them no longer have a negative impact on them because of the therapy.

The cognitive behavioural therapy assists the patient to think more positively, which reduces self-stigma. Also, the person begins to look differently at other people's opinion concerning them; they become less preoccupied with other people's views and opinions towards them. The individual who is affected by mental illness who gets cognitive behavioural therapy becomes less defensive with other people, increasing their participation in social activities. The person's self-confidence is boosted; there is a renewal of hope. All this helps in boosting the person's self-esteem, thus reducing self-stigma. There is also the computerised cognitive behavioural therapy, which an individual can do by themself at home through the guidance of a mental health practitioner.

There are various mental illnesses and disorders, that can be treated using cognitive behavioural therapy. They include anxiety disorder, depression, psychosis, schizophrenia among others. In treating anxiety disorders, the patients are exposed to those activities, objects, or situations of which they are afraid. The aim is for them to confront their fears and overcome them, which reduces public stigma as the individual learns how to manage and control some of their concerns and interacts positively with the society.

Image of the Cognitive Behavioural Therapy

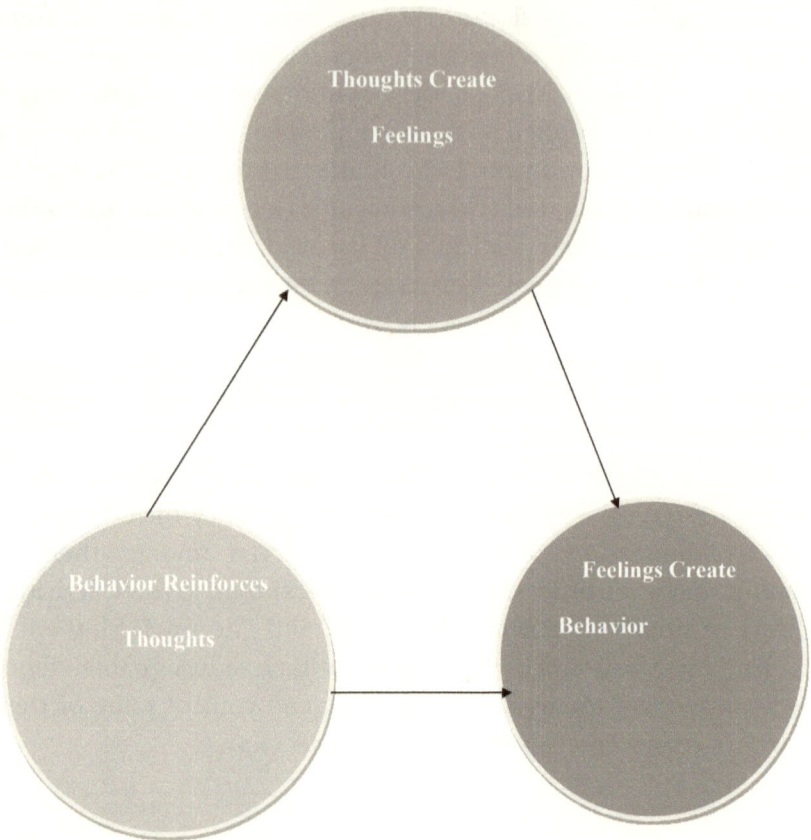

Psychotherapy

Psychotherapy assists the person who is affected by mental illness to understand themself more. During psychotherapy, the affected individual talks to a mental health professional who is trained to assist them in recognising the factors that trigger the illness. This therapy is helpful for those people affected by a mental disease which lasts for an extended period. Psychotherapy also assists those affected by mental illness to discern the feelings and behaviours that give rise to the illness and be trained on how to change them. During psychotherapy, the affected individual is assisted in identifying life's challenges that may be contributing to the illness and ways of solving them.

Life's challenges or problems include having a loved one in the family die and losing a job among others. As the individual learns on skills of solving problems, they regain control of their lives, which reduces self-stigma.

Dialectical Behaviour Therapy

The dialectical behaviour therapy is a talking therapy, mainly used by people who are affected by borderline personality disorder. The person who is affected by the disorder learns how to manage their behaviour and handle stressful situations. For people prone to behaviours which are harmful, they are trained on how to control these behaviours, leading to a reduction of self-harm. Dialectical behaviour therapy (DBT) can be conducted either on a one-to-one-session or in group sessions. The treatment through DBT can be conducted through four approaches, namely, skills training, a consultation team of therapists, coaching through phone, and individual treatment.

Training of Skills

During the skills training approach, the focus of the client is acquiring new skills and improving their abilities. The skills, which are the primary focus in this module, include regulating emotions, being able to tolerate distress, becoming efficient on an interpersonal level, and being mindfulness. In the skills training, open groups are most successful in comparison to individual sessions.

Consultation Team of Therapists

The consultation team comprises therapists or mental health practitioners who offer the dialectical behaviour therapy who meet periodically to consult on particular cases and to improve their skills as therapists.

Phone Coaching

There are patients or clients who may be prone to behaviours which are life-threatening. Counsellors or therapists may coach or train them over the phone when the need arises. Phone coaching can be done through proper laid guidelines.

Individual Treatment

A typical dialectical behaviour therapy is done on a weekly basis with the aim of enhancing the motivation of the client. The therapist conducting the personal treatment gives the client room to process thoughts which are not suicidal since the group programme is psychoeducational. There are various benefits which ensue as a result of the dialectical behaviour therapy; they include clients with various problems, such as stress, anxiety, adjustment disorders, benefitting from the skills offered. Also, this therapy can help in reducing stigma as the affected individual learns how to control self-harming behaviours which may have caused the person to experience discrimination and stigma from the public.

Creative Therapy

These are approaches to treating mental illness which is both creative and descriptive. The objective of creative therapy is to assist patients to get a way of expressing themselves which is beyond traditional therapy or words. This therapy comprises art therapy, music therapy, role play, and movement therapy. Creative therapy is used when a patient who is affected by mental illness is unable to take part in talk therapy. The people who are most suited for this kind of therapy are those who are unable to talk because of physical ailments, children, or those who are above the reach of language. Thus, it is beneficial to people who encounter difficulty in expressing themselves through the use of words.

During creative therapy sessions, the person who is mentally affected is guided on how to express themself through modelling with clay, painting, and drawing. The objective is to aid the person to connect with their emotions on various personal encounters. This kind of therapy is not limited to the session which the client has with the mental health professional; the client can continue with it when they are on their own or at home. An example of this is where the client can write at home in a journal concerning the feelings they may be experiencing; this helps in reducing stress and helps in focusing the individual's attention on a particular goal.

Creative therapy is beneficial for both children and adults since it is easy to implement and does not require hospitalisation or specific equipment. This therapy is helpful in reducing stigma since the emotions which the individual who is affected by mental illness is unable to express through words; they can do so through writing, drawing, or painting. By releasing suppressed emotions, the person can have an increase of energy as the sad feelings are lifted; thus, they are able to relate with those around them effectively. Through creative therapy, the person starts to accept themself, and the level of agitation decreases, and they can cope with day-to-day life. This tends to improve the relationship that they have with the other members of the society.

Exploring Facts as a Step in Reducing Stigma on Mental Illness

There are a lot of myths and misinformation which are associated with mental illness; these increase the stigma which is associated with the illness and those affected by it, together with their families. Some of the myths include the following: people affected by mental illness are violent and dangerous, these people should be treated as children, there is no recovery for people who have been affected by mental illness. Other myths state that mental health facilities are more harmful to the health of the affected individual and mental health professionals are sicker in comparison to their patients. Other myths or beliefs show that one can overcome mental illness through their willpower and being unable to overcome mental illness is a sign of weakness.

Reduction of stigma will come as a result of replacing these myths with facts; that is why it is necessary for people to have facts on mental illness causes, symptoms, and treatment. Some of the facts concerning mental illness include mental illness being brain disorders which are biologically based and one being unable to conquer them through willpower. These facts will assist in reducing the stigma associated with mental illness, especially in the Asian community which associate mental diseases with weakness (Kishore et al., 2011). Also, seeking treatment will not be considered as a sign of weakness but of strength (Lin & Cheung, 1999).

Another fact that will help in reducing stigma is that treatment is necessary for the recovery of the affected individual. The sick individual should not be hidden. An example is in the Asian community where a person who is affected by mental illness tends to be hidden from the public view, which further worsens the symptoms and makes treatment difficult. Media has misrepresented mental disease by implying that people from particular communities are more prone to mental illness than others. The fact is anyone can be affected by mental illness. By knowing this, the society will accept people who are affected by mental illness as they know anyone is prone to having the disease.

The media, at times, in their reporting or television shows tend to imply that mental illness is caused by a single factor. The fact is mental illnesses and disorders are caused by various factors which can be either biological, psychological, or environmental. The biological factors are hereditary; this is where a particular mental illness runs in the family. An example is bipolar disorder and schizophrenia which is genetic. Another biological factor is a prenatal injury during early development of the brain for a foetus when still in its mother's womb and which can cause mental illness. The environmental factors, on the other hand, refer to life stresses, such as financial challenges and unemployment. The psychological factors include death of a loved one; physical, emotional, and sexual abuse; and trauma.

There are myths which are propagated through media, which include mental illness being portrayed as a sign of creativity. An example is the movie concept, 'The charismatic psychopath is everywhere', where ladies affected by mental illness are depicted as charming. This myth is untrue since mental illness does not make an individual more creative; neither does receiving treatment diminish one's creativity. Some people hold on to the belief that mental illness is a product of a person's imagination and that it does not exist. The fact is, mental illness is not a product of a person's imagination or a way of seeking attention or even the failure of the person's character; instead, it is a real illness, just like any other physical ailment.

The people who are affected by mental illness have been portrayed as violent and dangerous; an example is those affected by schizophrenia (Goulden, 2011). Many crimes which are violent are linked to people who are affected by mental diseases. Because of this wrong portrayal, the society tends to distance themselves socially from these individuals out of fear. This is a misrepresentation since statistics show that the rate of violent crimes in the general public is similar to the one among people who are affected by mental illness. Knowing this can assist in dispensing this myth (Corrigan et al., 2012). In reality, there are many crimes committed by people who are not affected by mental illness (Monahan, 1996). Having these facts will lessen the public stigma towards people who are affected by mental illness.

People who are affected by mental illnesses and disorders can, at times, be hospitalised, but this is an exception and not the norm though the public believes that these people should be in hospitals. Having the knowledge that these people should be living at home with their love will reduce the stigma which they face in the society, where they are viewed as those who do not belong. In employment, the people who are affected by mental illness are perceived as being unable to work (Reavley & Jorm, 2011). Through treatment, a person who is affected by mental illness can work and live an ordinary life.

The right knowledge will help both employers and co-workers not to disease against these individuals in the workplace and treat them as equals. The stigma which causes those affected by mental illness to lack employment opportunities will reduce as they will be given an equal chance with those who are mentally healthy during the recruitment process (Alexander & Link, 2000). The affected person will not fear to disclose their mental condition since there will be no stigma attached to mental illness in the workplace. The employer will accord the necessary help required to those affected by mental illness; this can include giving them lighter duties during their recovery process and days off from work when they need to go for treatment.

Another fact that can help in reducing the stigma that is associated with mental illness in the society is it is possible to prevent mental illness from occurring. One way mental illness can be stopped is by ensuring a mother who has been diagnosed with mental illness; treatment is provided to her to limit the chances of passing the same to the unborn child. Another way of preventing mental illness is by avoiding substance abuse, especially among adolescents and youths, since substance abuse often leads to mental disorders.

Caregivers and the family of the person who is affected by mental illness need to realise that they play an essential role in the recovery process of this individual. Most people who surround the affected person feel and believe that they cannot do anything to help. When the individual is treated as an ordinary human being, they feel secure which, in turn, hastens their recovery as they are not experiencing stigma from the society and those around them. When handling a person who is affected by mental illness, one should treat them in the same way they would like others to treat them if they were in the same position.

There are cultures which associate mental illness to evil spirits or the sins of one's ancestors; an example is in South Asia. This kind of culture hinders people who are affected by mental illness from seeking treatment (Amri & Bemak, 2012, p. 50). This erroneous belief has deepened the stigma which the affected people experience as they tend not to seek treatment which worsens the illness. These cultural views should be discarded given the fact that mental illness affects the mind and has nothing to do with evil spirits or religious convictions. By embracing the fact that mental illness is not a result of evil spirits, those affected will seek early intervention, resulting in recovery and lessening of the public stigma.

Creating Coping Skills as a Step in Reducing Stigma on Mental Illness

Coping in psychology can be defined as the way in which an individual puts conscious determination to resolve problems which are either personal or interpersonal. The means of coping disease are referred to as coping skills or strategies. Coping skills can either be adaptive, which means skills that lessen stress, or be maladaptive, which means skills which can significantly intensify stress. When a person is first diagnosed with mental illness, they go through shock and intense emotional reactions, such as hopelessness, anger, and despair. Later some of those diagnosed come to accept the diagnosis; it is at this stage where they need to develop coping skills together with their families in order to manage the illness and reduce the stigma attached to the disease.

There are various adaptive coping skills which a person affected by mental illness, together with their family and caregivers, can develop to reduce the stigma that is associated with the mental diseases and disorders. These skills include looking for support from others, having an adequate sleep, thinking positively, communicating, focusing on other issues apart from the mental illness. Other adaptive coping skills or strategies include seeking information regarding the mental illness which the person has been diagnosed with and accepting the diagnosis. Some of these adaptive skills and their impact on reducing stigma on mental illness have been discussed below.

Seeking Social Support as a Coping Skill in Reducing Stigma on Mental Illness

Support groups have been significant in reducing the stigma which is attached to mental illness. An example of a support group is the National Alliance on Mental Illness (NAMI), which offers educative programmes on mental illness to both the affected person and their families. The Family-to-Family programme is a programme offered by NAMI, where the families who have one of them being affected by mental illness are trained through psychoeducation on how to relate to the affected individual. At times, the family members of the affected individual use strategies of avoidance to cope with the situation as they feel incapable of dealing with the issue at hand (Rammohan et al., 2002).

The burden of taking care of the person who is mentally affected may cause the family members to avoid them, either by leaving the individual physically or by declining to talk about the illness (Rammohan et al., 2002). Having access to social support, which is an adaptive coping skill, will assist the family in being able to handle the situation, which, in turn, will enhance the chances of recovery of the affected person, thereby reducing the stigma (Lazarus & Folkman, 1984). Some of the social support groups which the family and the affected person can use include friends, churches, educational institutions, extended family, and healthcare facilities.

Acceptance as a Coping Skill in Reducing Stigma on Mental Illness

Accepting the diagnosis of mental illness or disorder by both the affected person and their family is the first step towards their recovery process. Agreeing to a mental health diagnosis is difficult at the beginning as it signifies a health challenge. When an individual has been diagnosed with a mental illness or disorder, accepting the diagnosis becomes difficult because of the stigma associated with the disease (Corrigan et al., 2005). When both the family and the individual who has been affected by mental illness accept the situation, they tend to look at it positively. Acceptance helps to reduce stress in the family and aid in improving the relationship within the family. Consequently, the affected person does not suffer stigma within the family because of acceptance.

Communication as an Adaptive Coping Skill

Social stigma discourages family members from sharing or giving information to the public or people outside their family concerning their loved one who is affected by mental illness (Wenzke et al., 2004). Though communication can cause stigma, it can become an adaptive coping strategy since as the family seeks information from the mental health practitioners, they become better equipped on how to manage the situation. With the information that they get from the mental health practitioners and support groups, the family, together with the affected individual, can educate the public on mental illness. Educating the public or society, in turn, reduces the social stigma which the affected individual may be undergoing. The individuals who are affected by mental illness, together with their families, can also join advocacy groups to fight against social stigma by speaking out.

Sleep and Adequate Nutrition as Adaptive Coping Skills in Reducing Stigma on Mental Illness

Lack of sleep can cause worry and anxiety, further worsening the symptoms of the person affected by mental illness. An example is where people affected by anxiety disorder tend to experience more anxiety and fear because of sleep deprivation. Through having a regular sleep pattern, the affected individual can control the symptoms of the disorder, and some of them recover fully. Additionally, getting enough sleep for the person with bipolar disorder can assist in managing the depressive or manic episodes. Also, having adequate sleep results in better management of the symptoms of mental illness, such as anxiety and bipolar disorders. It can be viewed as an adaptive coping strategy.

As the symptoms become manageable and the individual begins their recovery process, the society can start becoming more accommodative of the person. This can reduce the social stigma which the individual with their family members may have been experiencing previously. Eating the right nutrition will prevent the affected individual from having other physical ailments, such as obesity, diabetes, and respiratory illness, which people affected by mental illness are predisposed to and which can put their health at risk (Social Exclusion Unit, 2004).

Reducing Stigma on Mental Illness through Gaining Mental Freedom and Acceptance

Accepting that one has been affected by mental illness is an essential process towards recovery. Accepting a medical or health diagnosis is difficult at first as it signifies a health challenge. When an individual has been diagnosed with a mental illness or disorder, accepting the diagnosis becomes difficult because of the stigma associated with mental illnesses (Corrigan et al., 2005). The person may fear that those around them will look at them differently or discriminate against them, especially in cultures where mental illness is a taboo topic (Corrigan et al., 2011). Another reason which hinders a person from accepting the diagnosis is the prevailing adverse attitudes in a particular community towards people affected by mental illness.

Also, those affected by mental illness may internalise the negative attitudes and words from their family and society, making them feel inferior in comparison to the other members of the society. The third factor that may cause the affected person not to accept their condition is the beliefs concerning the outcome of the illness; an example of one of the views is that there is no recovery for mental diseases (Deegan, 1988). Additionally, the label associated with a particular mental illness, such as schizophrenia, may cause the affected individual not to accept the illness.

Acceptance of the diagnosis will enable the person to understand that the illness is not their fault or that they are not responsible for their disease. This will reduce the self-stigma as the person realises that this is just an illness like any other and they are not being chastised because of their wrongdoing. Acceptance can also become a source of hope as the person looks for solutions for recovery. Accepting a mental illness diagnosis can result in a decrease in shame, fear of stigmatisation, and self-blame for the affected individual.

By accepting the diagnosis, the individual starts their treatment, accelerating their recovery process, thus reducing public stigma as the person can manage the mental illness symptoms. By understanding how the sickness influences their behaviour, the individual can take charge and change the way they relate with those around them. Change of behaviour will make the public to view those affected positively, reducing the stigma which they may have been experiencing. There are particular losses which a person who has been diagnosed with mental illness experiences; they include loss of hope, loss of confidence, loss of critical social responsibilities among others. The affected person needs to accept that they have suffered these losses and look for ways of overcoming and not internalising them to reduce both public and self-stigma.

People who are affected by mental illness face various limitations, which may be emotional, physical, and financial. The individual needs to accept their limitations and look for their strengths, which will aid them in looking for new opportunities in their lives. These opportunities may include making new friends, going back to school, and engaging in new activities within the community. In other words, the affected person should look at life positively and build up new values and goals which they can fulfil in the long run; doing this will diminish self-stigma. Accepting the diagnosis can help the person take responsibility for their recovery by adhering to treatment (Greenglass & Fiksenbaum, 2009).

Moreover, acceptance will make the affected person avoid situations that can trigger the illness, rendering the symptoms more manageable, and this will improve the person's quality of life. Accepting the diagnosis is not a sign of one's strength only, but also limitations. The person, rather than feeling ashamed of the limitations, feel proud that they can survive a destructive disease. To accept the mental illness diagnosis, the affected person needs to develop interpersonal methods of doing this, which involve interacting with people who are willing to give support to them without any prejudice. These people include mental health professionals, family, and peers.

The Acceptance Process

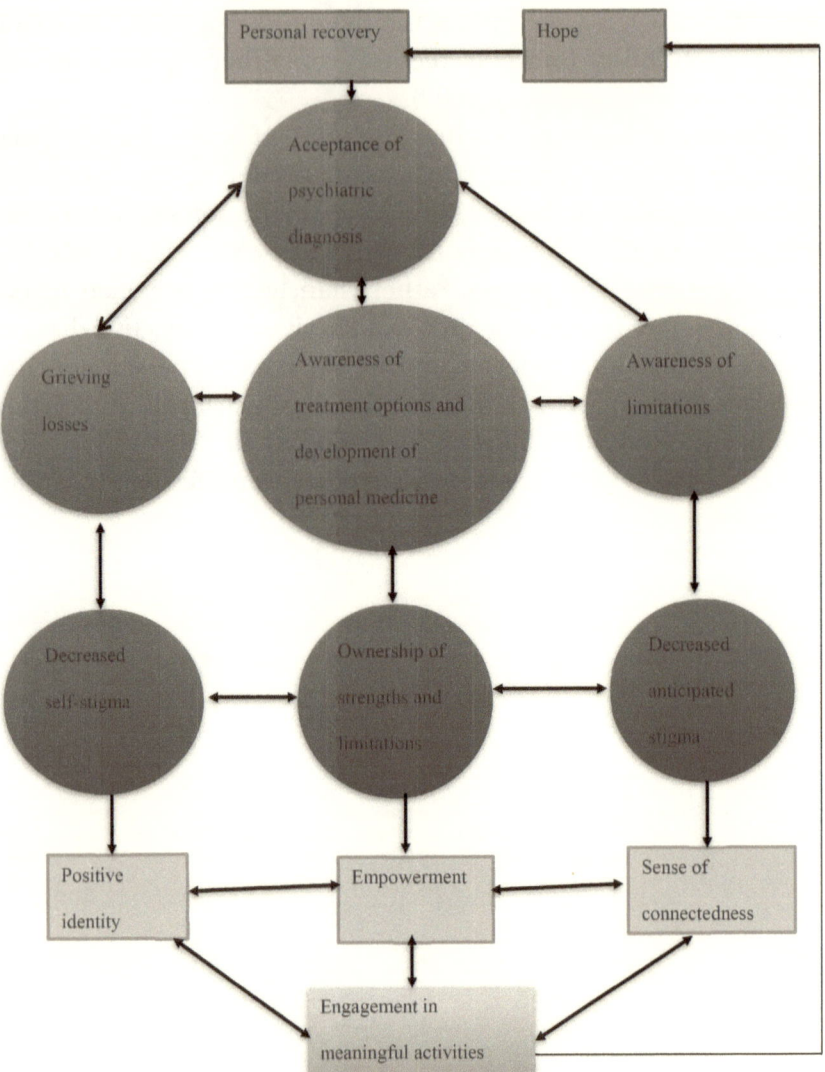

In concluding chapter 5, we will look at the various models which can be used in reducing the stigma which is related to mental illness. They include, among others, the conceptual model and the basic needs model. These two models have been discussed and illustrated below.

Conceptual Models in Reducing Stigma on Mental Illness

According to Samargia et al. (2006), 20 per cent of adolescents are affected by mental illnesses and disorders. As most of these cases are not managed during adolescence, they persist during adulthood (Kessler at al., 2005). By not treating the mental disorders when they occur in adolescence, those affected experience poor health later in their adulthood. Adolescents usually do not seek early treatment for mental illness because of the stigma which is attached to the disease. The adolescents want to fit in with their peers, such that they shy away from discussing mental health issues, to avoid being considered different from the rest (Hagan et al., 2008).

Attitudes and behaviours are formed early in life, that is, during adolescence and childhood, and they tend to shape how the way an individual will perceive things later in life (Wahl et al., 2007). Changing adolescents' behaviours and attitudes towards mental illness and those affected by it will encourage adolescents to seek early treatment. Change of attitude will bring cultural change among the adolescents, which will result in open discussions on mental illness among them, significantly reducing the stigma that is connected to mental illness.

Also, there are various anti-stigma campaigns which have been developed for adolescents. One of them is In Our Own Voice programme, which was designed by the National Alliance on Mental Illness; it has helped in lessening the stigma which is connected to mental illness among college students (Wood & Wahl, 2006). In Our Own Voice programme was established in 1996 with an objective of reaching out to people affected by schizophrenia and other mental illnesses. With time, the programme began to attract other people who were mentally healthy, which reduced significantly the stigma that is related to mental illness.

In Our Own Voice (IOOV) programme has four strategies used in decreasing the level of stigma on mental illness in the society. The first approach is putting a human face to mental illness. People who present during the IOOV programmes are those who are recovering from mental illness; they are regarded as human beings first, and being affected by mental disorder comes second. The second approach or strategy of IOOV is, illustrating different mental illnesses through videos and having people who are affected by mental illness share their experiences or personal stories. Through this approach, the audience widens their views about people affected by mental illness.

The third approach includes showing mental illness as being a disorder of the brain with a high biological element. The objective of this plan is to minimise the blame placed upon those affected by mental illness, where they are seen as being responsible for their status. The fourth strategy of IOOV focuses on the connection that exists between the treatment of mental illness and recovery, where presenters emphasise on the procedure of treatment first and then recovery through their stories. During the presentation, a person first states their name, what they do in life, and later their experiences with mental illness. Following this procedure helps the audience see the person as a human being first and not as a 'mentally ill patient'.

In Our Own Voice (IOOV) has been used in developing conceptual models of reducing the stigma of mental illness among the adolescents. An example is the model of research which has several constructs that include the learning, persuasion, and development stages as discussed below.

The Learning Stage

According to Paivio (1986), the dual coding theory is one used in learning where people are perceived to learn more when the information is both seen and heard. One of the tools that deliver information through dual coding is the television. Adolescents prefer watching television rather than reading information which is in print form (Walma et al., 2006). Thus, television through the use of positive stories from people affected by mental illness can be used to reduce stigma which is related to mental illness by providing accurate information.

Persuasion

Communication which is persuasive and where people have a choice among competing stories that can assist in establishing a description of history is referred to as narrative paradigm theory

(NPT) (Cragan & Shields, 1995). This theory comprises five assumptions, the first one being human beings are storytellers naturally and gain knowledge regarding the world by listening and telling stories. The second assumption which the narrative paradigm theory holds is that human beings judge what they hear through 'good reason', which means how consistent and coherent the story is and how true the story seems to the listener. The third assumption for NPT is that 'good reason' is influenced by an individual's character, beliefs, culture, and experiences.

The fourth assumption of the narrative paradigm theory is that a human being considers a story or narrative to be true if they can compare it to their own experiences or circumstances. The last assumption of the NPT is that a human being selects between the different stories to build and rebuild social reality as a continuous process. Through hearing stories, the listener changes their perception of mental illness, thereby reducing the stigma attached to the illness (Sandelowski, 1991). The stories can also guide the listener if they are affected by mental illness on how to intensify their recovery process.

The narrative paradigm theory, which is a part of the conceptual model, reduces stigma in three ways. The first is, the stories told include real-life experiences and values of the storytellers who may be similar to the person listening. The second way which stigma is reduced is that through NPT, all people, regardless of age, are capable of selecting and judging stories. The third way in which this theory contributes to the reduction of stigma on mental illness is that it is compatible with the current means of communication used by adolescents in their social network (Lerner & Steinberg, 2004).

Stage Development

Adolescents are perceived to be in the last stage of development of their lifespan according to Piaget's adaptation and equilibrium theory (1972). At this stage of life, the adolescent starts to think systematically, imagining how their current life impacts on their future. According to this theory, development happens when people get information from their surroundings or environment. Since children learn their first stories on mental illness through their environment, telling the corrects stories can expose children to accurate information on mental illness, reducing stigma that is associated with the illness (Hinshaw et al., 2003)

Image of a Conceptual Model of Reducing Stigma That Is Connected to Mental Illness

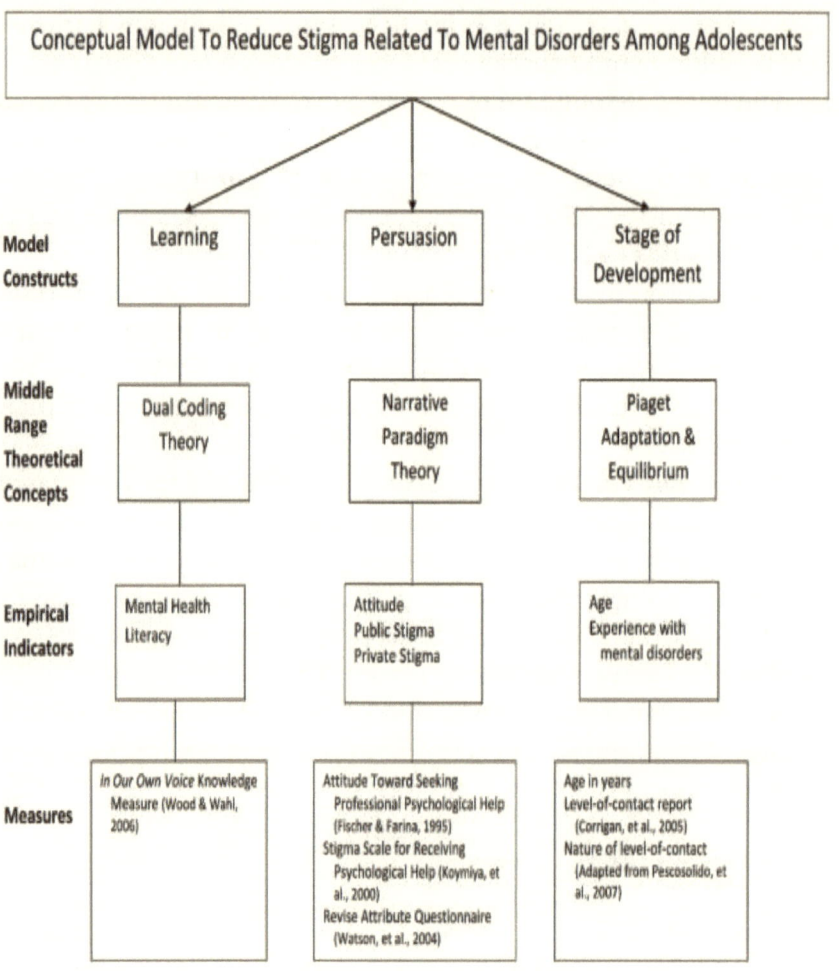

The Basic Needs Model

The basic needs model was developed in 1999 by Chris Underhill who received funding from Joel Joffe and Andrews Charitable Trust. The purpose of this model is to assist the people who are affected by mental illness not only to recover but also to build a livelihood which is sustainable. The programmes for basic needs are run in Asia, Australia, Africa, and Latin America. The model comprises five modules which consist of capacity building, sustainable livelihood, research, collaboration, and community mental health. The model incorporates those who are affected by mental illnesses and disorders in seeking solutions to their challenges. Participants are encouraged to join self-help organisations and groups to create opportunities which will support them on their journey of recovery. Since the community is involved in this model, the stigma is reduced as they all learn about mental illness. This model consists of a series of steps which are discussed below.

Capacity Building

This is where identification, mobilisation, sensitisation, and training on mental illness is done to the community and the government. Also, the person who is affected by mental illness is empowered to stand up and speak out for themself to lower the level of stigma associated with those affected by mental illness.

Community Mental Health

This is where affordable and effective community-based treatment of mental health is provided to the people who are affected by mental illness.

Sustainable Livelihoods

This module necessitates the need of developing a sustainable livelihood for the person affected by mental illness after their recovery. Those affected are provided with opportunities to work and earn to give back to their families and society. By encouraging the person to make their own livelihood, the person's independence is enhanced and they are able to resettle back in the society, this reduces stigma from the public which they may have been experiencing prior.

Research

In this module, the necessity of performing research on matters, such as shortage of some particular medication, as being a contributing factor to the hindrance in the recovery of people affected by specific mental illnesses is stressed.

Collaboration

Here, partnerships are formed with those who are involved in the execution of the model. In this module, activities of managing the available funds are done to guarantee these funds are distributed appropriately.

A practical example of how the basic needs model works is by supporting a mental health practitioner, such as a psychiatrist, to go into a particular community to implement mental healthcare in that community. After the patients have received treatment and recovered, they are requested to state the kind of work they would prefer; funds are given to them to enable them to have a sustainable livelihood. The work or activity which they choose should be appropriate for them; an example is where people who have seizures as a result of mental illness should not be permitted to work with machines that are heavy.

In cultures who value traditional healing methods in the treatment of mental illness—for example, the Latino community—the basic needs model can incorporate traditional healers (Luna, 2003). The model also educates the community through written materials on mental illness, with an objective of reducing the stigma that is attached to mental illness. This model incorporates the traditional, cultural, or religious healing methods of the particular community. The traditional and spiritual healers are taught on how to handle people who are affected by mental illness since these people seek their services first before seeking treatment from a mental health facility.

The Basic Needs Model of Reducing Stigma
That Is Connected to Mental Illness

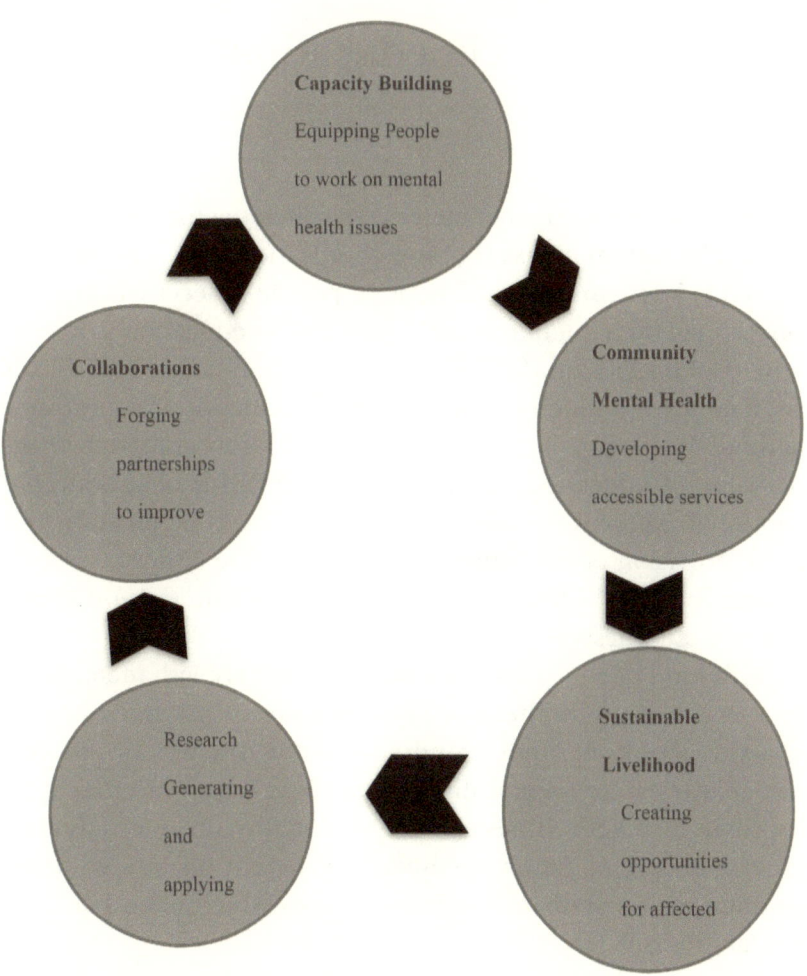

CHAPTER 6

Psychoeducation

There has been a significant increase in educating the people who are affected by mental illness (Landsverk & Kane, 1998). The reason for this is that it is a fundamental right for people to receive information concerning their mental health, and psychoeducation covers this right (Colom & Lam, 2005). Psychoeducation refers to a flexible-based education which integrates both therapeutic and educational methods in its approach. The psychoeducation approach realises the value of education in transforming harmful behavioural and emotional patterns. About mental illness, psychoeducation refers to the provision of education to people who are either receiving or looking for mental health services, which include those diagnosed with mental illnesses.

This kind of education does not deal entirely with mental illness since it is not psychotherapy. The objective of psychoeducation is to assist people in understanding mental diseases or disorders, particularly severe mental illnesses, such as schizophrenia, anxiety disorders, psychotic illnesses, and personality disorders. Both the patients and their family members are taught on how to develop communication skills and solve problems which arise because of mental illnesses.

Various tools are used during psychoeducation sessions, which include handouts for therapy and worksheets. This therapy is carried out by health professionals or any person who is an expert in the particular condition. The health professionals include social workers, nurses, physicians, psychologists, or trained health instructors. For psychoeducation to be successful, it needs to function under an open-door strategy, where patients can have visits which are unscheduled to the therapist when the need arises. Also, psychoeducation requires team effort for it to be a success. Various professionals are involved in the provision of psychoeducation; hence, they would need to work together as a team.

Psychoeducation is mostly associated with mental illness, where the person affected by mental illness is educated on the signs or symptoms, treatment, and diagnosis of the particular mental illness. Through psychoeducation, patients are empowered by the provision of tools which can assist them to handle and deal with the disease (Colom, 2011). It is not easy to understand mental illnesses, which often leads to discrimination and bias towards those affected and their families. To end the stigma which is attached to mental illness, it is imperative to understand the disease; this is necessary not only for people that have been diagnosed with mental illness but also for those who are mentally healthy.

Moreover, the relationship between the therapist and the patient should have a relationship whose basis is trust. Both the patient and the therapist should be open to accepting the treatment techniques which are suitable for the patient. Psychoeducation is offered depending on the particular mental illness. For example, for people affected by mental illness by depression, the psychoeducation should help them in acquiring skills that will assist them in solving problems. These people should also be educated on how to have positive thoughts and replace them with negative ones (Klausner, 1998). Moreover, people affected by schizophrenia, at times, can have problems with their concentration, attention, and memory (Emer at al., 2002). Thus, the psychoeducation should aim at improving their cognitive abilities (Hogarty, 2004).

For the psychoeducation to be successful, the information should be provided in a manner which is friendly to the participants. In most psychoeducation programmes, an unstructured format is mostly preferred. The reason for using the informal format is because most patients who attend psychoeducation are not able to concentrate for extended periods, and with the reduction in their attention level, the participants may end up becoming unmotivated.

The History of Psychoeducation

The term *psychoeducation* has been used for the most of the twentieth century, but it did not gain much popularity until the campaigns against mental illness stigmatisation began. The term was first used on the rate of relapse of adults who were affected by schizophrenia but has since evolved to include other mental illnesses (Birley & Wing, 1962). C.M. Anderson, an American researcher, can be associated with the development and popularisation of psychoeducation in 1980, where the term came into use on the background of providing treatment to people who were affected by schizophrenia (Anderson et al., 1980). The focus of the research conducted by C.M. Anderson was on educating the family members on the signs of schizophrenia, handling the person affected by mental illness, and managing stress arising within the family because of mental illness.

When the term *psychoeducation* was first used, its purpose was to illustrate a therapeutic concept whose focus was on behavioural change of the affected person; the family members were part of the therapy. Psychoeducation assists in taking away a person's confusion, fears, and other challenges regarding a mental illness diagnosis, which may hinder them in their treatment. Psychotherapy and psychoeducation are different; though the two terms are often confused, psychoeducation involves obtaining information, whereas psychotherapy entails applying the information gathered (Friedberg & McClure, 2002).

The psychoeducation model works with other theories, namely, the group practice theory, ecological system theory, cognitive behavioural theory, narrative approach theory, and the stress and coping model (Lukens & McFarlane, 2004).

Ecological System Theory

The ecological system theory gives the structure for evaluating and assisting individuals to understand their condition in connection with the other systems which are in their lives. The other systems include family, partners, school, peers, political systems, and the society among others. Psychoeducation can be provided in connection with the ecological system theory by adjusting it to fit families, groups, and individuals. Even though psychoeducation can be carried out on a one-to-one basis, group psychoeducation is more efficient since it assists in creating networks for the participants (Pennix et al., 1999). Group psychoeducation lessens isolation which occurs in the individual psychoeducation group.

The Ecological System Theory

Cognitive Behavioural Theory in Psychoeducation

The cognitive behavioural therapy is an organised approach whose objective is to tackle the problems which a patient could be experiencing currently (Dobson & Dobson, 2009). The emphasis of the cognitive behavioural theory is on the patient's way of thinking and its influences on both their behaviours and emotions (Ellis, 1994). The cognitive behaviour theory states that the pattern of thinking which an individual has is usually developed over time, depending on the individual's experiences while interacting with their environment (Beck, 1976). The beliefs, ideas, and assumptions which a person has impact on how they interact with the environment. The success of this theory depends on the participation of both the patient and the therapist.

The cognitive behavioural therapy targets particular symptoms and helps the patient on issues that involve their esteem and their functioning socially. This therapy enables the patients to learn how to manage their feelings to attain their goals. The cognitive behavioural therapy also empowers the affected individuals to get back control of their lives through the use of psychoeducation which uses various techniques that relate to the diagnosis of a specific individual. The cognitive behavioural therapy makes use of multiple methods in addressing the patient's problems. One of the techniques is psychoeducation, where cognitive behaviour therapy encourages the use of websites, videos, and books, which are moulded to fit the client.

The cognitive behavioural theory recommends that when a patient is receiving psychoeducation, the materials provided should be fitting to the patient's language, interests, education, and their need for privacy (Dobson & Dobson, 2009). Also, it helps the clients in identifying the particular problems which they may be experiencing and develops techniques of managing them. Problem-solving is a core component of psychoeducation; in the cognitive behavioural therapy, solving of the client's problem starts with the identification of a particular issue. The mental health practitioner or the therapist then looks at the factors which constitute the problem, which may include how often the problem occurs, what triggers the problem, and what techniques to be established to solve the problem.

For the duration of the process, the mental health practitioner encourages the client to contemplate changing. Also, the mental health practitioner, together with the patient, creates various techniques which can help in solving the problem. Each alternative is analysed by both the therapist and the patient and the possibility it has in solving the particular problem. The ideal approach is chosen, and its application is deliberated on in detail. An example is when it will be implemented, how it will be done, and how long it will last. The patient then applies the chosen approach as part of their homework.

Lastly, in looking for problem-solving approaches, the mental health practitioner and the patient assess the result of the strategy; if it was useful in solving the problem, they go to the following problem. If the approach has not assisted in solving the problem or addressed only a part of it, the mental health professional and the patient go back to the drawing board to look for other alternative approaches (Dobson & Dobson, 2009).

The cognitive behavioural therapy can work jointly with psychoeducation through the use of interventions which are exposure-based (Farmer & Chapman, 2008). The psychoeducation therapist will educate the patient on the purpose of confronting their fears, which is to lessen it. An example is people who are affected by the anxiety disorder being encouraged to face their fears, which helps in reducing its power. Exposure-based interventions should be done continuously and during and after the sessions, up until the fear is lessened.

Moreover, the cognitive behavioural therapy can assist a patient to realise the link that exists among their thoughts, feelings, and behaviours. The patient is trained through psychoeducation on how to identify the thoughts which are problematic by recording their thoughts. Recording of thoughts assists the patient to develop awareness of the thoughts which are harmful and share them with the mental health practitioner. After identifying the negative thoughts, the mental health practitioner and the patient develop alternative positive thoughts to replace the negative ones. The alternative thoughts, together with the original thoughts, are examined regarding their benefits. The patient is then assisted to learn to respond to their problem using their new thought pattern.

Group Practice Models in Psychoeducation

The psychoeducation which is provided through group models that comprise friends, family, and caregivers is more successful in comparison to when it is offered on an individual basis (Lamb et al., 2010). The reasons for the success of group models in psychoeducation are that the participants share their experiences and discover mutual ground and the members' feelings of isolation are lessened (Cogen & Graybeal, 2007). Through sharing of similar experiences, the participants' sense of empowerment is intensified (Pistrang, Barker, & Humphrey, 2008). The group practice model in psychoeducation has various benefits. One of the benefits includes the reduction of the patients' feelings of being alone in their problem as they meet with other people whom they are experiencing similar issues with.

A benefit which come as a result of the group practice model in psychoeducation is that the participants, especially those who are new to the group, experience a sense of belonging. The new members also experience a renewal of hope in facing the challenges which they may be experiencing in connection with mental illness as they see other members who are further along in their treatment process. The patients also learn new skills of managing the symptoms of mental illness from the training which they receive and from the experiences of others within the group. Group practice models are also beneficial to the patients since their stress level which emanates from isolation are reduced.

Furthermore, the patients have the chance to experience continuous learning within the group. Also, in the group, the members can be involved in various exercises which assist in developing socialising skills. Also, the group practice model offers social support to the participants; also, there is less stigmatisation within the group as the members share experiences and challenges. The patients' self-esteem, which may be low because of the stigma which they may have experienced in the society as a result of mental illness, is increased. The primary need of being understood is usually satisfied in group settings as the participants develop a feeling of connection with one another.

In the group setting, the participants can experience emotional healing through sharing with other members concerning their challenges. The members of the group can also benefit by imitating those in the group who have positive behaviours, including the therapist.

Narrative Approach Theory in Psychoeducation

Narrative theory is a type of psychotherapy which assists individuals to recognise their values. This theory begins by assuming that narratives are simple human techniques for coming to terms with essential parts of our experiences in life. Through this approach, the client is assisted in identifying the abilities and understanding which they have and can assist them in living their values to confront the challenges which they may be experiencing. In this approach, the therapist seeks to embrace a therapeutic position which aims at working as a team together with the client. The therapist listens, examines, and summarises the story of the patient's life.

The narrative approach theory aims at not combining a person's identity with the challenges they are undergoing or the errors they may have made in their lives. The slogan of the approach is 'The individual is not the problem, but the problem or challenge is the problem' (White & Epston, 1990). The client is requested by the therapist to name their problem or challenge to externalise further (Roth & Epston, 1996). Naming and externalising the problem is a technique used in the narrative approach theory to assist the patient in moving forward.

This approach also looks at an individual's convictions, abilities, ethics, and understanding as a means of assisting them in reclaiming their lives from a challenge or a problem. During the therapy, the mental health practitioner or therapist helps the client through questions to give voice to a problem by externalising it.

One of the goals of the narrative approach theory is to assist the client in sharing stories that they may be believing and holding on to, which may be hindering them from moving forward. Also, the therapy aims at recreating the opinion of the patient regarding themself and their environment. To draw out these stories from the clients, the therapist requires to both listen and ask the right questions. Both the therapist and the client need to talk about how the problem has impacted on the various parts of the patient's life. The therapist should assist the patient to pinpoint times before the problem occurred and recreate new stories based on these occasions.

After externalising their problem, the client is trained on how to talk about their new story with other people in the society (William, 2006). The approach is particularly beneficial to the people who are affected by various addictions or have experienced trauma in their lives. These people can be assisted in realising the impact of their problems and help them remember when they were free from the problem. Also, the person is empowered to plan for who they want to be and stop blaming themself for the problem.

The narrative approach theory can be used in connection with psychoeducation to remove the guilt and self-blame which some people affected by mental illness tend to have. For example, people who have co-occurring disorders because of substance abuse may experience guilt since they feel they have contributed to their current condition. The narrative approach theory, in connection with psychoeducation, can help the patient to put a distinction between the state they are in and their identity.

There are various benefits which accrue by using the narrative approach theory with psychoeducation in the treatment of mental illnesses and disorders. One of these benefits includes the client or patient being enabled to move from a mindset which is inactive, recognising that they have power over the challenges that they are going through (Nicholas, 2009). Another benefit of the narrative approach theory is that the patients stop blaming themselves for the problems since they can put a distinction between their identity and the problem.

The Stress and Coping Model in Psychoeducation

Integrating the stress and coping model in psychoeducation is necessary since it offers guidance to the mental health professionals to recognise the stressors which the patient has and how the patient responds to them to recommend styles of managing the stressors which are useful. Stress has been defined as a situation where the demands surpass the supply which an individual can marshal both socially and personally (Lazarus & Folkman, 1984). The environment which an individual lives in cannot define stress, but how the individual perceives and responds to the situation is what defines stress.

The stress and coping model can be used in psychoeducation, where the clinician assists the patient to consider the dynamics that significantly influence their reaction to stress, which is referred to as the cognitive appraisal. These factors include how threatening the stress seems to the individual and the evaluation of the resources which are needed to eradicate, lessen, or endure the stressor and the stress brings. The first stage of appraisal is the initial appraisal, where the patients, together with their families, learn to look at stressors not as threats but as challenges to be overcome.

In the secondary appraisal, the client learns to assess the coping alternatives which they have, which can be either external or internal. The internal options include their inner strength and willpower, while the external options can be their families, friends, peers, and health professionals.

Furthermore, the client learns how to cope with the mental illness; the mental health professional educates the patients to adopt the coping style which focuses on the problem. The problem-focused coping strategy helps the patient and their families to identify the challenge or problem, create substitute solutions, learn new ways of managing the stressors, and discover new behaviours. The coping style which focuses on emotions is discouraged in the psychoeducation programmes as it tends to make the client avoid or distance themself from their problems.

A Stress and Coping Model

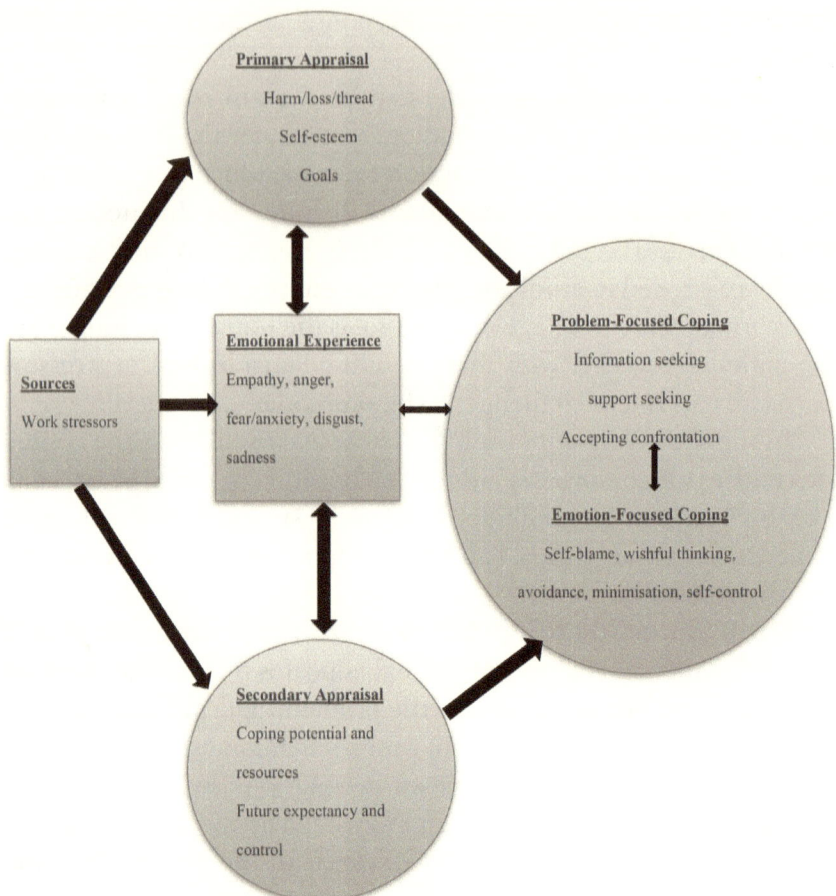

Psychoeducation Approaches

Psychoeducation is the initial step in alleviating the anxiety which comes with a mental illness diagnosis. The fear is lessened when the mental health practitioner gives adequate information in a manner which is understandable and at the correct time. Learning can be aided by the provision of information in various ways. An example is when the participants are encouraged to write notes of what they are learning or are given information in written form. The mental health practitioner conducting the psychoeducation programme, when required, should repeat the information. The participant should be encouraged to talk about their fears openly; this can be achieved by having the therapist ask open-ended questions, such as if they are in pain, or what their worst fear is.

Psychoeducation is offered depending on whether the programme is for the person who is affected by mental illness or if it entails members of their family and caregivers. Regarding the medical part of psychoeducation, the participants learn how the disease may impact them physically later in their lives and how to change their minds to think positively. The participants also learn about ways to manage and reduce the stigma that is linked to mental illnesses. The patient, together with the family, also learns how stigma impacts on their lifestyles and self-esteem.

Furthermore, psychoeducation offers information on the treatment which the patient or client may be receiving. The information which is given answers various questions regarding the treatment, for example, 'How does the treatment work?', 'What are the advantages of using the medication?', 'What are the adverse side effects of the medication?', and 'Why should the drugs be used at particular times?' During the sessions, the different types of psychotherapies which are accessible and appropriate for the patient and their families are discussed. Additionally, the participants learn whether there is any financial assistance which is available to them.

The patients who have a disorder whose cause is substance abuse tend to feel guilty and responsible for their condition. Psychoeducation assists these patients to understand that what has happened is in the past and they need to learn ways in which to manage their current situation.

Common Topics in Psychoeducation

There are various topics which are covered in psychoeducation; they include, among others, the health features of the mental illness, where the condition is identified and defined. Also, the patient learns how the disease may limit them physically in the future. Another subject which is looked into is the stigma which is associated with the particular mental illness and ways that can be done to fight it. Additionally, the members learn about healthy lifestyle actions to assist them to manage the disease. The patients also learn the importance of adhering to the treatment schedule to hasten their recovery process and avoid any relapse.

Objectives/Goals of Psychoeducation

There are various goals and objectives of psychoeducation; they include, among others, making sure that the family members of the person who is affected by mental illness get the necessary training which will enable them to be competent when providing care to the affected individual. Another goal is to assist the family and caregivers to make informed decisions when managing the mental illness. Another objective of psychoeducation is to train the patient to become an expert of their illness grows. Furthermore, the family members are empowered to become co-therapists during the treatment procedure.

The Importance/Benefits of Psychoeducation

Psychoeducation offers many benefits to both the person who is affected by mental illness and their family members. For example, it raises the awareness of mental illness, which helps those who are affected to accept their condition and to seek for treatment. Additionally, psychoeducation assists in ending social stigma; Stigmatisation can cause people who are affected by mental illness to avoid treatment, further worsening the symptoms and the disease. Additionally, psychoeducation can help prevent a relapse as the patients are taught on how to detect early signs of a relapse. The self-esteem of the patients who receive psychoeducation is impacted positively, enabling the individual to become self-sufficient. Since psychoeducation teaches techniques of solving problems to both the affected individual and their family, these individuals develop feelings of empowerment.

Various studies have been conducted on the benefits that accrue from psychoeducation; an example is a study conducted in Canada, whose focus was the people who are affected by bipolar disorder (Michalak et al., 2005). The objectives of the study were to help the patients in identifying the signs the disorder, increase their knowledge of the disorder, and improve their understanding of the treatments which are available. Furthermore, the patients were educated on the strategies of coping with the disorder. There were many benefits which came as a result of psychoeducation, which included a significant improvement in the patients' quality of life.

Another study was conducted in New York concerning the response to psychoeducation of adults affected by depression (Klausner et al., 1998). The result showed a considerable decrease in the symptoms of depression which the patients experienced previously. Moreover, the patients seemed to be more hopeful, less anxious, and socially functional. The people affected by schizophrenia who have taken part in psychoeducation report significant improvement in complying with the medication routine. Furthermore, these individuals receive a better knowledge of the mental illness and acquire skills that help them adjust to life.

During psychoeducation, the patients are taught on healthy practices and lifestyles; an example is having an adequate sleep, eating a balanced diet, and exercising, which is essential for people with mental disorders, such as bipolar and anxiety disorders. The people who are affected by mental illness also learn to keep away from substance and alcohol abuse to avoid co-occurring conditions (Drake et al., 1991). Because of behavioural changes, the patients are hospitalised fewer times; they have an enhanced adherence to medication, and the quality of their lives improves.

Psychoeducation helps in preventive relapses since both the patient and their family receive training on how to track the early signs of a relapse. The knowledge which the family gains concerning mental illness helps improve the quality of their lives since they learn on ways of solving problems which arise because of having one of them affected by mental illness. The family receives training on the side effects of the medications which the affected individual is using, which helps them know how to treat the person when they are experiencing the adverse side effects. Another benefit of psychoeducation is that there is a reduction on the stigma which the person who is affected by mental illness goes through as the community learns on mental illness.

The Categories of Psychoeducation

Psychoeducation sessions can be conducted through discussions performed on a one-to-one basis or individual discussions in different family groups or with a particular family, such as psychoeducation for caretakers and friends, peer-to-peer psychoeducation, and social psychoeducation (Razali, 1997). These are discussed below.

Individual Psychoeducation

Individual psychoeducation focuses on the particular patient's circumstance; the information provided by the therapist is precisely for that patient. Psychoeducation can be divided into some sessions. During the first meeting, the patient is directed to sit facing the educators to facilitate eye contact. The therapists or educators introduce themselves to the patient; later, the patient is asked to introduce themself. The information concerning the intention and period of the programme is provided to the patient by the educators. After that, the affected individual is requested to share their experiences regarding their illness; the educators then give information concerning the disease to the patient. The patient's expectations during the therapy are noted down by the educators.

During the second session, the patient learns how to avert a relapse by having emergency plans in place. The person who is affected by mental illness learns how to identify early signs indicating the start of the disease. The third session can involve the educator teaching the patient on the side effects of the medication which may be used to control the symptoms of the illness and on ways to manage them. A fourth session can also be conducted, where the patient is educated on communication skills and on various ways in which they can solve problems which they face on a day-to-day basis. Patients who get anxious in group settings are suited for individual psychoeducation since they do not feel intimidated.

Group Psychoeducation

Group psychoeducation is useful for the patients who attend to feel they are receiving support from the other group members; this reduces the anxiety that the patient may be experiencing because of the illness. Additionally, participants in the group share their experiences; this helps everyone to learn on how to deal with their conditions through other people's experiences (Ascher & Whitesel, 1999). The participants receive information through interacting with their peers in the group who may be experiencing similar issues. Group psychoeducation can last for one year to some years.

Group discussions require a leader who believes that the people affected by mental illness can learn, receive information, and have the capability to have productive lives. This leader will then communicate the positive values and beliefs to the participants (Hayes & Gants, 1992). The participants in the group want to feel that the leader understands their mental illness and is capable of guiding them through their vulnerable situation. The discussions can be done through videotapes or handouts; the members should be encouraged to participate. It is imperative to involve the participants in selecting and planning the content which will meet their exact needs. It is important to note that group psychoeducation can include either a single-family psychoeducation or multifamily group discussions.

Family Psychoeducation

Family psychoeducation, which was developed by M. J. Goldstein and David J. Miklowitz, is a means of working with caregivers, families, and friends who take care of the person who is affected by mental illness (Goldstein & Miklowitz, 1990). Educating the person who is affected by mental illness is not enough; the family members who bear the most burden need to be taught about it too. Consequently, psychoeducation programmes for the entire family are necessary; this will assist in reducing the burden and stress which arise as a result of taking care of the affected person. The family psychoeducation can be provided for either a single family or some families together; the aim is to help in building better relationships within the family. This therapy can be executed for several families at the same time. The family psychoeducation can be conducted in a social background or setting, away from a mental health facility.

Most families living with an individual who is affected by a mental illness are often critical and unsupportive to the sick individual. At times, the family members alienate the individual who is affected by mental illness because of lack of knowledge of their role in the person's recovery process (Lefley, 2009). Family psychoeducation helps in educating the family members on their role and responsibility regarding their loved one who is affected by mental illness. Family psychoeducation has proved to be more efficient than when it is done on an individual basis according to research done in China. The rate of relapses in individual psychoeducation is higher compared to family psychoeducation (Hogarty et al., 1997).

The research was conducted on sixty-nine people affected by schizophrenia and eight people affected by psychosis in four months. The patients were assigned randomly to two treatment states, that is, family psychoeducation and individual psychoeducation. The people who got the intervention together with their families had considerable changes in comparison to those who received treatment as individuals. The changes comprised a high level of compliance with treatment, and low levels of neglecting and abusing the patient within the family were reported. Additionally, there was a significant improvement of the mental state of the participants who were affected by mental illness.

Family psychoeducation emphasises developing communication skills and skills which they are to use when solving various problems. Some of the benefits of psychoeducation include family members increasing their knowledge of mental illness and their health which may have been affected by the strain of taking care of their loved ones. Both the person who is affected by mental illness and their family are engaged and requested to participate in the treatment process; they become participants rather than spectators in the recovery process of the affected individual. An example of family psychoeducation is the family-to-family programme which is offered by the National Alliance on Mental Illness (NAMI) in the United States of America.

Goals of Family Psychoeducation

Family psychoeducation has various goals, among them being the reduction of symptoms of mental illness in the affected person. Additionally, this therapy helps in the prevention of frequent hospitalisations and relapses. For those patients who require rehabilitation, family psychoeducation encourages them to be rehabilitated as either inpatients or outpatients. Furthermore, the family members' capacity is capitalised to help in promoting the recovery of their loved one. Psychoeducation is also helpful in managing crisis and preventing people who are affected by mental illness from taking away their lives.

Benefits of Family Psychoeducation

There are various benefits associated with family psychoeducation; they include the prevention of a relapse of the person who is affected by mental illness (Zoladl et al., 2007). Also, it helps in improving communicating skills within the family. Furthermore, the family gains information on the particular mental disease which their loved one has which reduces their burden as they learn to take care of them. Psychoeducation can also result in lowering the stress levels within the family, which often arise as a result of having to take care of a person who is affected by mental illness within the family. Furthermore, the information which the family receives can assist them in developing better communication methods or techniques within the family.

The Benefits of Family Psychoeducation

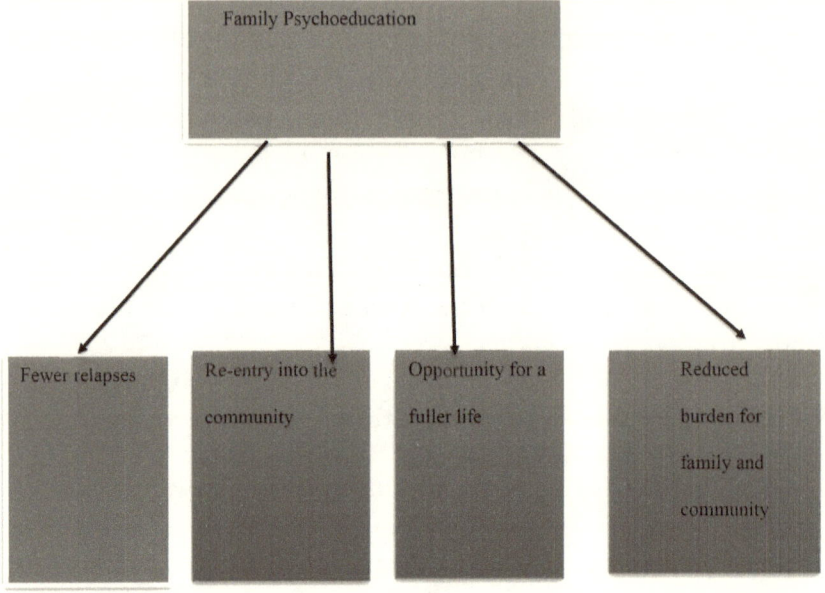

Components of Family Psychoeducation

There are various elements which comprise family psychoeducation; they include joining, educating, establishing problem-solving strategies, creating a favourable recovery environment, and forming support and social groups.

Joining

The health practitioner sets up a relationship with both the patient and the family members which is helpful, trusting, and respectful. The relationship should include cultural values which the family hold for it to be successful. An example is in the Asian countries where the permission of the family is required by the mental health professional for them to treat the person affected by mental illness. The purpose for this is to assist the practitioner in understanding the patient's family cultural views concerning the origin of the disease and their expectations are regarding treatment.

Educating the Family on the Particular Mental Illness

People tend to fear what they do not understand. By providing education to the family members concerning the particular mental illness which has affected their loved one, this fear will be dispelled. Facts will dispel many myths which the family members may be having about mental illness, which can include that it is dangerous living with the person (Corrigan et al., 2001). The affected may be desiring contact with family members and friends which they rarely receive as the family is afraid of mental illness. Psychoeducation will assist in minimising instances where the person who is affected is isolated from family members.

Establishing Methods for Solving Problems

The practitioner or therapist works with the patient and the family to develop strategies which will assist them in managing complicated circumstances which may arise because of mental illness in the family. Some of the techniques which the practitioner can train the family to use during the problematic situations include using behavioural, communicative, and cognitive techniques. An example is the cognitive behavioural therapy which assists the affected to change how they think and behave since this is connected to how they feel. This therapy looks at how one's childhood experiences have affected their behaviour. Since the cognitive behavioural therapy targets specific symptoms, it will assist the patient with issues that involve their esteem and their functioning socially. This therapy will help the patient to understand how their thoughts affect their reactions to different situations.

Creating a Favourable Recovery Environment

An optimal environment is necessary for enhancing the treatment and recovery of an individual who is affected by mental illness. The practitioner in family psychoeducation works together with the family to ensure that the home environment which they live in is conducive to enhancing quick recovery for the affected individual.

Creating of Support Groups

In most cases, the practitioners carry out the treatment in groups of families. In these groups, families share their experiences in handling an individual who is affected by mental illness. Thus, support groups are essential during the affected person's recovery process (Stroul, 1989). The group offers the affected individual encouragement as they can share freely their challenges and successes. Support groups are helpful in managing various mental illnesses; an example is the obsessive-compulsive disorders as the individual shares on their fears with the other members.

Significant Features of the Family Psychoeducation

For the family psychoeducation to be effective, various components should be available, namely, education on mental illness, problem-solving, the duration which is long-term, reduction of stress, and involvement of the family.

Education on Mental Illness

Mental illness education comprises giving information to the family concerning the likely cause of the illness and the side effect of the medication which the patient could be using. Also, psychoeducation can also recommend or offer rehabilitation services for those who may require.

Problem-solving

The families who attend the family psychoeducation programmes learn techniques or methods of solving various problems which arise as a result of having one of them being affected by mental illness.

Reduction of Stress

The person who is affected by mental illness, jointly with the members of their family, learn how to manage stress. Through learning stress reduction techniques, the family's confidence in taking care of their loved one improves, which, at times, may avert a crisis within the family.

Extended Period

Psychoeducation services are provided as long as the family requires them. Some families may be needing the services for a shorter time in comparison to others. Hence, the family psychoeducation is modified to meet individual family needs.

Family or Client's Involvement

Members of the family or the person affected by mental illness should be present during the training of family psychoeducation.

Barriers to Implementing the Family Psychoeducation

There are various obstacles which can hinder putting into practice or implementing family psychoeducation. These hindrances include mental health practitioners lacking sufficient time to meet the goals of the participants (Fadden, 2006). Another barrier can be health practitioners not having adequate training which is required to handle family psychoeducation. Furthermore, the mental health practitioners may be unable to have a schedule which is flexible to carry out the psychoeducation sessions.

Additionally, the family members may experience barriers that may hinder them from attending the psychoeducation sessions (Fadden, 1997). Some of the challenges include transport and planning when to attend the sessions. The psychoeducation meetings may also seem to add to the demands which the family members may be having, which makes it difficult for them to be consistent in attending the sessions. Moreover, the stigma associated with mental illness may prevent the family from attending the psychoeducation programmes. The family may not want the society to know that their loved one is affected by mental illness, which may lead them hiding their loved one rather than attending the psychoeducation programmes. The family members may not be at ease disclosing the issues they may be having as a family, which hinders them from attending the psychoeducation sessions (Drake et al., 2001).

The Stages of a Family Psychoeducation Therapy

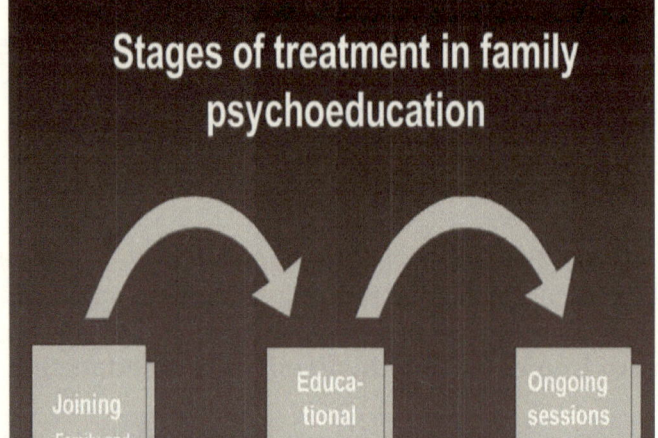

Psychoeducation for Caregivers and Friends

Many of the adults who are affected by mental illness have no family to offer them support. Thus, they tend to rely on friends and caregivers. The caregivers who take care of the adults or children who are affected by mental illness experience a lot of stress and anxiety as the illness in most instances is prolonged and challenging. In the long run, the caregivers may become emotionally exhausted and experience burnout because of isolation, stigma, and discrimination which are linked to mental illness. There are the caregivers who take care of more than one patient at a time. In the beginning, the caregivers may have hope that the person will recover, but when it does not happen, their hope dwindles.

At times, the occupation of the caregivers tends to be adversely impacted since there are times when the caregivers may need leave from work to take care of the sick person. The employer may want to know the reason for their absence, and on explaining, the caregiver may start to experience stigma and discrimination in the workplace. Hence, it is imperative that the caretakers and friends receive psychoeducation to learn how to handle these situations (Coon et al., 2003). Psychoeducation focuses on enhancing the understanding of the caretaker on the behaviour of the person who is affected by mental illness.

The caregivers may require information on the mental illness which has affected the person of whom they are taking care of (Biegel, 1995). Thus, the caretakers and friends should be educated during the psychoeducation sessions on how to take care of the personal challenges which they could be having and which could be hindering them from adequately taking care of the affected individual (Aldrich, 2011). In circumstances when the affected individual is absent, the caregivers learn through psychoeducation the nature of the mental illness affecting their loved one. The ways of identifying the symptoms and triggers of the disease are also taught during psychoeducation. The caregivers also learn the steps to take during emergencies, and in case there is any social, legal, and financial support, the caregivers learn about it.

Peer-to-Peer Psychoeducation

According to Rummel et al. (2005), who came up with this approach, peer-to-peer- psychoeducation involves people who have undergone a particular experience currently helping those in the same condition. Those who have had a particular challenge and overcome it are in a better position to empathise with those who may be having a similar challenge or problem. The ex-patients are referred to as peer moderators and can encourage the patients during the psychoeducation sessions. According to Rummel et al. (2005), there are five stages of peer-to-peer psychoeducation.

The first step is where the peer moderators participate in the programme where a trained mental health practitioner is the one conducting it. The peer moderators are expected to give information to people who have just been affected by mental illness, together with their families or caregivers. In the second step, stage workshops which offer training are conducted with the guidance of the mental health practitioner. The peer moderators receive knowledge on various mental illnesses and disorders and ways to conduct and handle the activities of a group. The training at this stage is usually done through video presentations and a particular manual developed precisely for the peer moderators.

In the third stage, the moderators are requested to carry out the programme of the group for the participants or patients. The mental health practitioners may be in attendance, but they only participate in the programme when requested. In the fourth stage, the peer moderators are called upon to carry out the psychoeducational programmes independently, while the mental health practitioner's participation is passive. In the final step or phase, new peer moderators are recruited, the patients who have recovered and who may be interested in making available the information they have received to other patients and their family members can be recruited.

Multifamily Groups Psychoeducation

The multifamily group psychoeducation refers an intervention based on evidence where people who are affected by mental illness receive psychoeducation, together with their families. In the multifamily psychoeducation groups, there are different families who are involved. They include those who receive education on mental illness, support by the family, how to intervene during a crisis and useful strategies in communication (McFarlane, 2002).

The multifamily psychoeducation comprises three stages. In the first phase, the mental health practitioner or the therapist conducts a workshop to educate the different families. The focus of the workshop is to teach the family on ways of preventing relapse and promote both occupational and social rehabilitation. In the second phase, the various families are trained on how to work together as a community. The third stage is where there are conscious attempts at shaping the families into a community system which will continue for an extended period and be able to support one another socially.

During the multifamily group's first session, the members are encouraged to share on subjects which are not connected to mental illness, which can include their day-to-day activities and their likes and dislikes. This kind of sharing enables the families to get to know one another and to find out general concerns and interests. The multifamily psychoeducation programmes are based on the fact that the families who are trying to manage mental illness face a lot of challenges which dishearten them. With time, the family members become excessively critical towards the affected individual.

For the duration of the family psychoeducation meetings, the issues on stigmatisation, social segregation, increase in both the psychological and financial burdens which the family could be experiencing are addressed. The group deals with this by enlarging the size of the community-support network and by linking the families who have similar challenges together. In the groups, the families share their experiences with others who have gone through same challenges and have gotten solutions or answers which are realistic and practical. The multifamily psychoeducation educates the families on executing the multifamily psychoeducation guidelines, developed earlier to reduce the stress which they could be experiencing.

Benefits of Multifamily Psychoeducation

There are many gains which arise when a family who has one of them being affected by mental illness attends the psychoeducation programmes. The benefits include the reduction of rate of relapse as the family knows about identifying early symptoms of a relapse. Also, the burden of caring for their loved one is significantly reduced since the family may receive financial aid and obtain the skills to care for the person who is affected by mental illness (Falloon et al., 1999). An example of patients having reduced rates of relapses are studies done on adults who were affected by schizophrenia who attended programmes on multifamily psychoeducation. The results indicated lowered rates of hospitalisation and relapse in comparison to patients who participated in the individual psychoeducation programme (Falloon et al., 1999).

The Models of Psychoeducation

There are different types of psychoeducation models. They can be grouped into four (Zipple & Spanial, 1997). The models include the information model, supportive model, skill-training model, and comprehensive model.

Information Model

This model emphasises the provision of knowledge to families concerning mental illness and its management. The objective of this approach is to enhance the awareness of families regarding the particular disease and how they can manage it.

Skill-Training Model

The purpose of the skill training model is to develop particular behaviours to enable the members of the family to build their capability in helping their loved one who is affected by mental illness more effectively.

Supportive Model

The supportive model uses support groups which are intended to develop and enhance the emotional capability of the family in managing the burden of taking care of their loved one who is affected by mental illness.

Comprehensive Model

This model is a combination of the information, supportive, and skill models. In the preliminary stage of this model, the participants are taught about mental illness. The members are expected to participate in a multifamily support group. In the closing stage, the members are required to participate with a mental health professional as participants of individual sessions (Leff et al., 1992).

CONCLUSION

This book has endeavoured to write in detail concerning mental illnesses, their causes, symptoms, treatments, and stigmas. The purpose of this book is to help reduce the stigma that is connected to mental illness in the society. The media has been seen as a significant tool that can help in the reduction of stigma on mental illness through conveying accurate information. There are laws and regulations which have been enacted to reduce the stigma against people who are affected by mental illnesses, but there should be emphasis that these laws be adhered to.

Though much has been done in reducing the stigma in various countries, more still needs to be done. The governments of various nations need to form social policies that will help educate the public on mental illness, with the aim of eradicating the stigma associated with the disease. There should be firm ways of dealing with people or organisations who knowingly stigmatise or discriminate against the people who are affected by mental illness in the society.

Various advocacy bodies, such as the National Alliance on Mental Illness, have been discussed, with the roles which they played in educating the public on mental illness. The call that is there is for more organisations to be formed with an aim of providing information regarding mental illnesses. The last chapter has been dedicated to discussing psychoeducation and its significance to the patient, their families, and the caregivers. People who are affected by mental illness should seek psychoeducation since it will help improve the quality of their lives and reduce the rate of relapse. Moreover, psychoeducation has been found to reduce the burden of the caregivers as they learn how to manage the stressors which come as a result of taking care of mental illness.

REFERENCES

Abu-Ras, W. M., and Suarez, Z. E. (2009). Muslim men and women's perception of discrimination, hate crimes, and PTSD symptoms post 9/11. *Traumatology, 15*, 48–63. http://dx.doi.org/10.1177/1534765609342281

Aldrich, N. CDC seeks to protect health of family caregivers. http://www.chronicdisease.org/nacdd-initiatives/healthy-aging/meeting-records/HA_CIB_HealthofFamilyCaregivers.pdf/view. Accessed 24 March 2011.

Alexander, L. A. & Link, B. G. (2003). The impact of contact on stigmatizing attitudes toward people with mental illness. *Journal of Mental Health*, 12(3), 271–289.

Aloud, N. & Rathur, A. (2009). Mental health and psychological services among Arab Muslim populations. *Journal of Muslim Mental Health, 4*, 79–103. http://dx.doi.org/10.1080/15564900802487675

Altarriba, J. & Bauer, L. M. (1998). Counseling the Hispanic client: Cuban Americans, Mexican Americans, and Puerto Ricans. *Journal of Counseling and Development, 76*(4), 389–396.

Amri, S. & Bemak, F. (2012). Mental health help-seeking behaviors of Muslim immigrants in the United States: Overcoming social stigma and cultural mistrust. *Journal of Muslim Mental Health*, 7(1), 43–63.

Anderson, C. M., Gerard, E., Hogarty, G. E., & Reiss, D. J. (1980) Family treatment of adult schizophrenic patients: A psycho-educational approach. *Schizophrenia Bulletin*, 6490–505.

Ascher-Svanum, H. & Whitesel, J. (1999). A randomized controlled study of two styles of group patient education about schizophrenia. *Psychiatric Services, 50*, 926–930.

Australian Bureau of Statistics. (2009). *National health survey 2007–08.*

Aviram, R. B., Brodsky, B. S., & Stanley, B. (2006). Borderline personality disorder, stigma, and treatment implications. *Harvard Review of Psychiatry, 14*(5), 249–256. doi:10.1080/10673220600975121

Bassett, J., Lloyd, C., & Bassett, H. (2001). Work issues for young people with psychosis: Barriers to employment. *British Journal of Occupational Therapy, 64*(2), 66–71.

Beiser, M. (1999). *Strangers at the gate: The 'boat people's' first ten years in Canada.* Toronto(ON): University of Toronto Press.

Biegel, D., Song, L., & Milligan, S. (1995). A comparative analysis of family caregivers' perceived relationships with mental health professionals. *Psychiatric Services, 46*, 477–82.

Bolton, J., Cox, B., Clara, I., & Sareen, J. (2006). Use of alcohol and drugs to self-medicate anxiety disorders in a nationally representative sample. *The Journal of Nervous and Mental Disease, 194*(11), 818–825.

Browne, G. & Courtney, M. (2007). Schizophrenia housing and supportive relationships. *International Journal of Mental Health Nursing, 16*(2), 73–80.

CAIR. (2006). *Western Muslim minorities: Integration and disenfranchisement.* Retrieved on 15 August 2010, from http://www.cair.com/Portals/0/pdf/policy_bulletin_Integration_in_the_West.pdf

CAIR. (2010). *About Islam and American Muslims.* Retrieved on 1 September 2010, from http://www.cair.com/AboutIslam/IslamBasics.aspx

Canada's ethnocultural mosaic, 2006 census. Ottawa (ON): Statistics Canada; 2008. 2. Populati.

Carers UK. (2014.) *Carers at breaking point*. London: Carers UK.

Carolan, M. T., Bagherinia, G., Juhari, R., Himelright, J., & Mouton-Sanders, M. (2002). Contemporary Muslim families: Research and practice. *Contemporary Family Therapy, 22,* 67–79. http://dx.doi.org/10.1023/A:1007770532624

Castel, J. M., Laporte, J. R., Reggi, V., Aguirre, J., Buschiazzo, P. M., Coelho, H. L., . . . & Fuentes, J. (1997). Multicenter study on self–medication and self–prescription in six Latin American countries. *Clinical Pharmacology and Therapeutics, 61*(4), 488–493.

Chaumba, J. (2011). Health status, use of health care resources, and treatment strategies of Ethiopian and Nigerian immigrants in the United States. *Social Work in Health Care, 50,* 466–481.

Chen, A. & Kazanjian, A. (2005). Rate of mental health service utilization by Chinese immigrants in British Columbia. *Canadian Journal of Public Health, 96,* 49–51.

Chirumbolo, A., Mannetti, L., Pierro, A., Areni, A., & Kruglanski, A. W. (2005). Motivated closed-mindedness and creativity in small groups. *Small Group Research, 36*(1), 59–77.

Chung, I. (2010). Changes in the sociocultural reality of Chinese immigrants: Challenges and opportunities in help-seeking behaviour. *International Journal of Social Psychiatry, 56,* 436–447.

Chung, R. C. Y. & Bemak, F. (2012). *Social justice counseling: The next steps beyond multiculturalism*. Thousand Oaks, CA: Sage.

Cohen, M. & Graybeal, C. (2007). Using solution-oriented techniques in mutual aid groups. *Social Work with Groups, 30*(4), 41–58.

Colom, F., Vieta, E., Sánchez-Moreno, J., Martínez-Arán, A., Reinares, M., Goikolea, J. M., & Scott, J. (2005). Stabilizing the stabilizer: Group psychoeducation enhances the stability of serum lithium levels. Bipolar Disorders

Commonwealth Department of Health and Aged Care. (2000). *Promotion, prevention and early intervention for mental health – A monograph*, 109. Mental Health and Special Programs Branch, Commonwealth Department of Health and Aged Care, Canberra.

Contextual and compassionate analysis. (cover story). *Australian and New Zealand.*

Coo, D. W, Thompson, L., Steffen, A., Sorocco, K., Gallagher Thompson, D. (2003). Anger and depression management: Psychoeducational skill training interventions for women caregivers of a relative with dementia. *Gerontologist, 43*, 678–689.

Corrigan, P. & Penn, D. (1998). Lessons from social psychology on discrediting psychiatric stigma. *American Psychologist, 54*, 765–776.

Corrigan, P. W., Powell, K. J., & Michaels, P. J. (2013). The effects of news stories on the stigma of mental illness. *Journal of Nervous and Mental Disease, 21*(3), 179–182. doi:10.1097/NMD.0b013e3182848c24

Corrigan, P. (2004). How stigma interferes with mental health care. *American Psychologist, 59*(7), 614.

Corrigan, P. W. (2002). Empowerment and serious mental illness: Treatment partnerships and community opportunities. *Psychiatric Quarterly, 73*(3), 217–228. doi:10.1023/A:1016040805432

Corrigan, P. W., Vega, E., Larson, J., Michaels, P. J., McClintock, G., Kryzanowski, R., & Buchholz, B. (2013). The California schedule of key ingredients for contact-based antistigma programs. *Psychiatric Rehabilitation Journal, 36*(3), 173–179.

Choi, S., Park, K., Woo, S., Kang, S., & Ra, J. (2014). Treatment of progressive supranuclear palsy with autologous adipose tissue-derived mesenchymal stem cells: A case report. *Journal of Medical Case Reports, 8*, 79–87.

Cragan, J. & Shields, D. (1995). *Symbolic theories in applied communication research: Bormann, Burke and Fischer.* Hampton Press: Cresskill, NJ.

Crisp, A. (2001). The tendency to stigmatise. *The British Journal of Psychiatry, 178*(3), 197–9. doi: 10.1192/bjp.178.3.197.

Crisp, A. H., Gelder, M. G., Rix, S., Meltzer, H. I., & Rowlands, O. J. (2000). Stigmatisation of people with mental illnesses. *British Journal of Psychiatry, 177*, 4–7.

Diefenbach, D. & West, M. (2007). Television and attitudes toward mental health issues: Cultivation analysis and the third-person effect. *Journal of Community Psychology, 35*, 181–195. doi: 10.1002/jcop.20142

Dietrich, S., Herider, D., Matschinger, H., & Angermeyer, M. C. (2006). Influence of newspaper reporting on adolescents' attitudes toward people with mental illness. *Social Psychiatry and Psychiatric Epidemiology.*

Dobson, D. & Dobson, K. S. (2009). *Evidence-based practice of cognitive-behavioral therapy.* New York, NY: Guilford Press.

Dobson, K. S. (Ed.). (2010). *Handbook of cognitive-behavioral therapies* (3rd ed.). New York, NY: Guilford Press.

Drake, R. E. & Wallach, M. A. (1989). Substance abuse among the chronic mentally ill. *Psychiatric Services, 40*(10), 1041–1046.

Drake, R. E., McLaughlin, P., Pepper, B., & Minkoff, K. (1991). Dual diagnosis of major mental illness and substance disorder: An overview. *New Directions for Mental Health Services, 50*, 3–12.

DRC. (2006). *Equal treatment: Closing the gap. A formal investigation into physical health inequalities experienced by people with learning disabilities and/or mental health problems.* Disability Rights Commission, London.

Ebrahimi, H., Namdar, H., & Vahidi, M. (2013). Mental illness stigma among nurses in psychiatric wards of teaching hospitals in the northwest of Iran. *Iranian Journal of Nursing and Midwifery Research, 17*(7), 534–8.

Falloo, I. R. H., Held, T., Coverdale, J., Roncone, R., & Laidlaw, T. (1999). Psychosocial interventions for schizophrenia: A review of long-term benefits of international studies. *Psychiatric Rehabilitation Skills, 3*, 268–290. 55. Baucom DH, Shoham V,

Farone, D. W. & Pickens, J. (2007). The mental health system and sense of self among adults with serious mental illness. *Journal of Human Behavior in the Social Environment, 15*(4), 35–54. doi: 10.1300/J137v15n04_03

Filaković, P., Degmecić, D., Koić, E., & Benić, D. (2007). Ethics of the early intervention in the treatment of schizophrenia. *Psychiatria Danubina, 19*, 209–15. PMID: 17914322.

Finkelstein, J., Lapshin, O., & Wasserman, E. (2008). Randomized study of different anti-stigma media. *Patient Education and Counseling, 71*(2), 204–214.

Flores, G. (2005). The impact of medical interpreter services on the quality of health care: A systematic review. *Medical Care Research and Review, 62*, 255–99.

Fox, Z. (2012). *Even in 2012, more Americans own TVs than cellphones.* Retrieved from http://mashable.com/2012/01/06/cellphones-tv-ownership/

Freeman, H., Wahl, O., Jakab, I., Linden, T.R., Guimón, J., & Bollorino, F. (2001). Forum - Mass media and psychiatry: Commentaries. *Current Opinion in Psychiatry, 14*(6), 529–535.

Friedberg, R., & McClure, J. (2002). Clinical practice of cognitive therapy with children and adolescents. *Journal of Developmental and Behavioral Pediatrics, 23*(6), 457–458.

Gaissmaier, W. & Gigerenzer, G. (2012). 9/11, Act II: A Fine-grained Analysis of Regional Variations in Traffic Fatalities in the Aftermath of the Terrorist Attacks. *Psychological science* (in press).

Gallo, J., Ryan, S., & Ford, D. (1999). Attitudes, knowledge, and behavior of family physicians regarding depression in late life. *Archives of Family Medicine, 8*(3), 249–256.

Gerbner, G., Gross, L., Morgan, M., Signorielli, N., & Shanahan, J. (2002). Growing up with television: Cultivation processes. In J. Bryant & D. Zillmann (Eds.), *Media effects: Advances in theory and research (pp. 43–68).* Mahwah, NJ: Lawrence Erlbaum Associates.

Gonzales, L., Davidoff, K. C., Nadal, K. L., & Yanos, P. T. (2015). Microaggressions experienced by persons with mental illnesses: An exploratory study. *Psychiatric Rehabilitation Journal, 38*(3), 234–241. doi:10.1037/prj0000096

Goulden, R., Corker, E., Evans-Lacko, S., Rose, D., Thornicroft, G. & Henderson, C. (2011). Newspaper coverage of mental illness in the UK, 1992–2008. *BMC Public Health, 11*, 796.

Gureje, O., Lasebikan, V. O., Ephraim-Oluwanuga, O., Olley, B. O., & Kola, L. (2005). Community study of knowledge of and attitude to mental illness in Nigeria. *British Journal of Psychiatry, 186*, 436–441.

Hackler, A. H., Cornish, M. A., & Vogel, D. L. (2016). Reducing mental illness stigma: Effectiveness of hearing about the normative experiences of others. *Stigma and Health, 1*(3), 201–205. doi:10.1037/sah0000028

Haley, A. & Malcolm, X. (1987). *The autobiography of Malcolm X.* New York, NY: Random House Publishing Group.

Hoffner, C.A. & Cohen, E.L. (2012), Responses to obsessive compulsive disorder on monk among series fans: Parasocial relations, presumed media influence, and behavioral outcomes. *Journal of Broadcasting and Electronic Media, 56*(4), 650–668.

Hogarty, G., Kornblith, S., Greenwald, D., et al. (1997). Three-year trials of personal therapy among schizophrenic patients living with or independent of family, I: Description of study and effects on relapse rates. *American Journal of Psychiatry*, 154.

Hogarty, G., Flesher, S., Ulrich, R., Carter, M., Greenwald, D., Pogue-Geile, M., Kechavan, M., Cooley, S., DiBarry, A., & Garrett, A., (2004). Cognitive enhancement therapy for schizophrenia: Effects of a 2-year randomized trial on cognition and behavior. *Archives of General Psychiatry, 61*, 866–876.

Holman, L. (2011). Building bias: Media portrayal of postpartum disorders and mental illness stereotypes. *Media Report to Women, 39*, 12–19.

Islam M. R. & Hewstone M. (1993). Dimensions of contact as predictors of intergroup anxiety, perceived out-group variability, and out-group attitude: An integrative model. *Personality and Social Psychology Bulletin, 19*(6), 700–710.

Jenkins, R., Bhugra, D., Bebbington, P., Fryers, T., Brugha, T., Farrell, M., Coid, J., Weich, S., Singleton, N., & Melzer, H. (2008), Debt, income and mental disorder in the general population. *Psychological Medicine, 38*, 1485–93.

Jorm, A., Korten, A., Jacomb, P., Christensen, H., & Henderson, S. (1999). Attitudes towards people with a mental disorder: A survey of the Australian public and health professionals. *Australian and New Zealand Journal of Psychiatry, 33*(1), 77–83. 10.1046/j.1440-1614.1999.00513.x.

Journal of family therapy, 25(4), 188–197.

Stengler-Wenzke, K., Trosbach, J., Dietrich, S., & Angermeyer, M. C. (2004). Coping strategies used by the relatives of people with obsessive-compulsive disorder. *Issues and Innovations in Nursing Practice, 48*(1), 35–42.

Kaplan, M., Adamek, M., & Calderon A. (1999). Managing depressed and suicidal geriatric patients: Differences among primary care physicians. *Gerontologist, 39*(4), 417–425.

Katon, W. & Schulberg H. (1992). Epidemiology of depression in primary care. *General Hospital Psychiatry, 14*(4), 237–247.

Kessler, R., Foster, C., Saunders, W., & Stang, P. (1995). Social consequences of psychiatric disorders, I: Educational attainment. *American Journal of Psychiatry, 152*(7), 1026–1032.

Khantzian, E. J. (1987). The self-medication hypothesis of addictive disorders: Focus on heroin and cocaine dependence. In *The cocaine crisis* (pp. 65–74). Springer, Boston, MA.

Kishore, J., Gupta, A., Jiloha, R. C., & Bantman, P. (2011). Myths, beliefs and perceptions about mental disorders and health-seeking behavior in Delhi, India. *Indian Journal of Psychiatry, 53*(4), 324–329.

Klausner, E., Clarkin J., Spielman, L., Pupo C., Abrams, C., Abrams, R., & Alexopoulos, G. (1998). Late-life depression and functional disability: The role of goal-focused psychotherapy. *International journal of geriatric psychiatry, 13*, 707–716.

Klin, A. & Lemish, D. (2008). Mental disorders stigma in the media: Review of studies on production, content, and influences. *Journal of Health Communication, 13*, 434–449. doi: 10.1080/10810730802198813

Kuo, B. C. H., Kwantes, C. T., Towson, S., & Nanson, K. M. (2006a). Social beliefs as determinants of attitudes toward seeking professional psychological help among ethnically diverse university students. *Canadian Journal of Counselling, 40*(4), 224–241.

Kwong, K., Chung, H., Cheal, K., et al. (2013). Depression care management for Chinese Americans in primary care: A feasibility pilot study. *Community Mental Health Journal, 49*, 57–165.

Lazarus, R. S. & Folkman S. (1984). Stress, appraisal, and coping. Springer, New York, NY, USA.

Leff, J., Kuipers, L., Berkowitz, R., Eberlein-Vries, R., & Sturgeon, D. (1992). A controlled trial of social intervention in the families of schizophrenic patients. *British Journal of Psychiatry, 141,* 121–134.

Lefley, H. P. (2009). *Family psychoeducation for serious mental illness.* Oxford University Press, New York, USA.

Lerner, R. M. & Steinberg, L. (2004). *Handbook of adolescent psychology* (2nd ed.). John Wiley & Sons Inc.: New Jersey.

Levitt, M., Lane, J. & Levitt, J. (2005). Immigration stress, social support, and adjustment in the first postmigration year: An intergenerational analysis. *Research in Human Development, 2*(4), 159–177.

Lewis-Fernandez, R., Das, A., Alfonso, C., et al. (2005). Depression in US Hispanics: Diagnostic and management considerations in family practice. *Journal of the American Board of Family Practice, 18,* 282–96.

Lin, K. M. & Cheung, F. (1999). Mental health issues for Asian Americans. *Psychiatric Services, 50,* 774–780.

Lorenzo-Blanco, E. I. & Delva, J. (2012). Examining lifetime episodes of sadness, help seeking, and perceived treatment helpfulness among US Latino/as. *Community Mental Health Journal, 48,* 611–626.

Luna, E. (2003). Las quecuran at the heart of Hispanic culture. *Journal of Holistic Nursing, 21*(4), 326–342.

Lyons, M., & Ziviani, J. (1995). Stereotypes, stigma, and mental illness: Learning from fieldwork experiences. *American Journal of Occupational Therapy, 49*(10), 1002–1008.

McGinty, E., et al. (2013). Effects of news media messages about mass shootings on attitudes toward persons with serious mental illness and public support for gun control policies. *American Journal of Psychiatry 1, 170*(5), 494–501.

Mental Health Council of Australia. (2005). Not for service: Experiences of injustice and despair in mental health care in Australia, Canberra.

Miklowitz, D. & Goldstein, M. (1990). Behavioral family treatment for patients with bipolar affective disorder. *Behavior Modification, 14,* 457–489.

Lewis-Fernandez, R., Das, A.K., Alfonso, C., et al. (2005). Depression in US Hispanics: Diagnostic and management considerations in family practice. *Journal of the American Board of Family Practice, 18,* 282–96

Moreno, F.A., Chong J., Dumbauled J., et al. (2012) Use of standard webcam and internet equipment for telepsychiatry treatment of depression among underserved Hispanics. *Psychiatric Services, 63,* 1213–1217

Moses, T. (2014). Stigma and family. In P. Corrigan (Ed.), *The stigma of disease and disability: Understanding causes and overcoming injustices* (pp. 247–268). Washington, DC: American Psychological Association.

Nichols, M. P. (2009). *The essentials of family therapy* (4th ed.). Boston, MA: Pearson Education.

Olstead, R. (2002). Contesting the text: Canadian media depictions of the conflation of mental illness and criminality. *Sociology of Health and Illness, 24*(5), 621–643. http://www.blackwellsynergy.com/links/doi/10.1111/1467-9566.00311/abs/

Overton, S. L. & Medina, S. L. (2008). The stigma of mental illness. *Journal of Counseling and Development, 86*(2), 143–151. doi:10.1002/j.1556-6678.2008.tb00491.x

Paivio, A. (1986). *Mental representations.* Oxford University Press; New York.

Penn, D.L., Chamberlin, C., & Mueser, K.T. (2003). Effects of a documentary film about schizophrenia on psychiatric stigma. *Schizophrenia Bulletin, 29*(2), 383–391.

Perlick, D. A., Nelson, A. H., Mattias, K., Selzer, J., Kalvin, C., Wilber, C. H., Huntington, B., Holman, C. S., & Corrigan, P. W. (December 2011). In our own voice-family companion: Reducing self-stigma of family members of persons with serious mental illness. *Psychiatric Services, 62,* 1456–1462. PMID 22193793. doi:10.1176/appi.ps.001222011.

Pescolido, B., et al. (2013). The 'backbone' of stigma. *American Journal of Public Health, 103*(5), 853–60

Pew Research Center. (2007). Muslim Americans: Middle class and mostly mainstream. Retrieved on 20 August 2010, from http://pewresearch.org/assets/pdf/muslim-americans.pdf

Pew Research Center. (2011). Muslim Americans: No sign of growth in alienation or support for extremism. Retrieved on 6 May 2013, from http://www.people-press.org/2011/08/30/muslim-americans-no-signs-of-growth-in-alienation-or-support-for-extremism/

Pistrang, N., Barker, C. & Humphreys, K. (2008). Mutual help groups for mental health problems: A review of effectiveness studies. *American Journal of Community Psychology, 42,* 110–121

Porter, M. & Haslam N. (2005). Predisplacement and postdisplacement factors associated with mental health of refugees and internally displaced persons: A meta-analysis. *JAMA, 294,* 602–12.

Rameela, A. & Hashim, I. H. M. (2004). *Nurses attitude towards the mentally ill in Indira Gandhi memorial hospital, Maldives.* Thesis submitted to University Sains Malaysia.

Rammohan, A., Rao, K., and Subbakrishna, D. K. (2002). Religious coping and psychological wellbeing in carers of relatives with schizophrenia. *Acta Psychiatrica Scandinavica, 105*(5), pp. 356–362.

Rao, D. & Valencia-Garcia, D. (2014). Stigma across cultures. In P. Corrigan (Ed.), *The stigma of disease and disability: Understanding causes and overcoming injustices* (pp. 283–296). Washington, DC: American Psychological Association.

Ratzliff, A. D. H., Ni, K., Chan, Y. F., et al. (2013). A collaborative care approach to depression treatment for Asian Americans. *Psychiatric Services, 64,* 487–490.

Reavley, N. & Jorm, A. (2011). *National survey of mental health literacy and stigma.* Commonwealth of Australia.

Reitmanova, S. & Gustafson, D. L. (2008). "They can't understand it": Maternity health and care needs of immigrant Muslim women in St. John's, Newfoundland. *Maternal and Child Health Journal, 12,* 101–111. http://dx.doi.org/10.1007/s10995-007-0213-4

Ridgway, P. (2001), Restorying psychiatric disability: Learning from first person recovery narratives. *Psychiatric Rehabilitation Journal, 24*(4), 335–4.

Roe, D., Lysaker, P. H., & Yanos, P. T. (2014). Overcoming stigma. In P. Corrigan (Ed.), *The stigma of disease and disability: Understanding causes and overcoming injustices* (pp. 269–282). Washington, DC: American Psychological Association.

Rog, D. (2004). The evidence on supported housing. *Psychiatric Rehabilitation Journal, 27*(4), 3.

Rose, D. (1998). Television, madness and community care. *Journal of Community and Applied Social Psychology, 8*(3), 213–228. http://www3.interscience.wiley.com/cgi-bin/abstract/5654/ABSTRACT

Rosenfield, S. (1997). Labeling mental illness: The effects of received services and perceived stigma on life satisfaction. *American Sociological Review, 62*(4), 660–72.

Saguy, A. & Gruys, K. (2010). News media constructions of overweight and eating disorders. *Social Problems, 57,* 231–250.

Samargia, L., Saewyc, E., & Elliott, B. (2006). Foregone mental health care and self-reported access barriers among adolescents. *Journal of School Nursing, 22*(1), 17–24.

Sandelowski, M. (1991). Telling stories: Narrative approaches in qualitative research. Image: *Journal of Nursing Scholarship, 23*, 161–166.

Schanie, C. F. & Sundel, M. (1978). A

Sirey, J., Bruce, M., Alexopoulos, G., Perlick, D., Raue, P., Friedman, S. J., et al. (2001). Perceived stigma as a predictor of treatment discontinuation in young and older outpatients with depression. *American Journal of Psychiatry, 158*, 479–81. PMID: 11229992.

Stier, A. & Hinshaw, S. P. (2007). Explicit and implicit stigma against individuals with mental illness. *Australian Psychologist, 42*(2), 106–117.

Stout, P. A., Villegas, J., & Jennings, N. A. (2004). Images of mental illness in the media: Identifying gaps in the research. *Schizophrenia Bulletin, 30*, 543–561.

Stroul, B. A. (1989). Community support systems for persons with long-term mental illness: Conceptual framework. *Psychosocial Rehabilitation Journal, 12*(3), 9.

Stuart, H. (2006). Media portrayal of mental illness and its treatments: What effect does it have on people with mental illness? *CNS Drugs, 20*(2), 99–106.

Tellier, C., & Felizardo, V. (2011). *Out of sight, back into mind: Federal offenders with mental disorders preparing for release into the community.* Presentation to the Canadian Criminal Justice Association Pan-Canadian Congress (October 2011). Retrieved on 4 August 2012, from www.ccia-acip.ca/cong2011/2011-G.pptx

Thompson, M. M., Naccarato, M. E., Parker, K. C. H., & Moskowitz, G. B. (2001). The personal need for structure and personal fear of invalidity measures: Historical perspectives, current applications, and future directions. In G. B. Moskowitz (Ed.), *Cognitive social psychology: The Princeton symposium on the legacy and future of social cognition* (pp. 19–41). Mahwah, NJ: Erlbaum.

Thornicroft, G., Rose, D., & Mehta, N. (2010). Discrimination against people with mental illness: What can psychiatrists do? *Advances in Psychiatric Treatment, 16*, 53–59. 10.1192/apt.bp.107.004481.

Torrey, W., Mueser, K., McHugo, G., & Drake, R., (2000). Self-esteem as an outcome measure in studies of vocational rehabilitation for adults with severe mental illness. *Psychiatric Services, 51*(2), 229–233.

Tolin, D. F. (2007). Descriptive impulse control disorders. *Cognitive Behavioural Therapy, 36*, 121–139.

Valdez, C. R., Padilla, B., Mcardell, M., & Magana, S. (2013). Feasibility, acceptability, and preliminary outcomes of the Fortalezas Familiares intervention for Latino families facing maternal depression. *Family Process, 52*, 394–410.

Waghorn. G. & Lloyd C. (2005). The employment of people with a mental illness: A discussion document prepared for the Mental Illness Fellowship of Australia.

Wahl, O., Hanrahan E., Karl, K., Lasher, E., & Swaye, J. (2007). The depiction of mental illness in children's television programs. *Journal of Community Psychology, 35*(1), 121–133.

Watson, A., Corrigan, P., Larson, J., & Sells, M. (2007). Self-stigma in people with mental illness. *Schizophrenia Bulletin, 33*(6), 1312–1318.

White, M. & Epston, D. (1990). *Narrative means to therapeutic ends.* New York: W. W. Norton.

Williams, N. (2006). Narrative family interventions. In A. Kilpatrick & T. Holland (Eds.), *Working with families: An integrative model by level of need* (4th ed.). Boston, MA: Pearson Education.

Wittmann, D., & Keshavan, M. (2007). Grief and mourning in schizophrenia. *Psychiatry: Interpersonal and Biological Processes, 70*(2), 154–16.

Young, J., Bailey, G., & Rycroft, P. (2004). Family grief and mental health: A systemic,

Zoladl, M., Sharif, F., Ghofranipour, F., et al. (2007). Common lived families with mentally ill patient: A phenomenological study. *Iranian Journal of Psychiatry and Clinical Psychology, 12*, 67–70.

INDEX

A

addiction   78, 110-11
alcohol   22-5, 66, 107-9
American Psychiatric Association
     21, 34, 37
American Psychological
     Association (APA)   158, 223
amphetamines   11, 23
Anderson, C. M.   184
anorexia   61, 71, 141
antisocial personality disorder   39
anxiety   7, 9, 11, 16-19, 25-9, 31, 39,
     47, 73, 75, 100, 103, 108-9,
     114, 124, 130, 164, 171, 192,
     197, 204
anxiety disorders   15-16, 18-19, 26-
     7, 48, 71-2, 109, 145, 161, 171,
     182, 195
avoidant personality disorder   38

B

bipolar disorder   10, 15, 19-22, 27,
     42, 54, 65, 73, 76, 85, 108,
     111, 122-3, 160, 166, 171, 195

C

Change Our Minds   158
cocaine   23, 34, 107-8, 112

cognitive analytical therapy (CAT)
     159
cognitive behavioural theory   184,
     186
cognitive behavioural therapy
     (CBT)   18, 26, 29, 36, 40,
     114, 159-61, 185-7, 201
cognitive closure   101-6
coping   168-73
counselling   159
creative therapy   159, 164-5

D

dependent personality disorder   38
depressants drugs   108
depression   10, 14-15, 21, 26, 43, 48,
     60, 62, 72, 74-5, 95, 98, 100,
     110-11, 118, 125, 127-8, 130,
     135-7, 146, 151, 160-1, 183, 195
depressive attack   20
disorders   40, 159, 163-4

E

early intervention   116-18, 120-5,
     139-41, 147, 150, 168
ecological system theory   184-5
electroconvulsive therapy   7-8, 36
etiological theories   2
exposure and response prevention
     (ERP)   29

F

family psychoeducation 197-200, 202-3

family therapy 36, 114-15, 160

G

group psychoeducation 197

H

hallucinogens 23

Hippocrates (physician and Greek philosopher) 5-6

histrionic personality disorder 38

hypomanic attack 20

I

impulse control disorder 40

K

Kraepelin (psychiatrist) 6

M

magnetic resonance imaging (MRI) 13

manic attack 20

marijuana 23, 26, 34, 107-8, 110, 112

mental illness, cultural beliefs and traditions, Asian American immigrants 126-7, 133-4, 137, 220, 223

mesenchymal stem cells (MSCs) 14, 215

methamphetamine 23, 107

Mindframe National Media Initiative 100

N

narcissistic personality disorder 38

narrative approach theory 184, 189-90

narrative paradigm theory (NPT) 176-7

narrative theory 189

National Alliance on Mental Illness (NAMI) 150, 152, 169, 198

O

obsessive-compulsive disorder 10, 15, 26-8, 30-1, 38, 65, 73, 75, 114, 142, 202

opiates 108

P

paediatric autoimmune neuropsychiatric disorder (PANDA) 10

panic disorder 16

paranoid personality disorder 40

psychoeducation 36, 133, 169, 182-8, 190-6, 198-9, 201-2, 204-6, 208

psychogenic theory 2

psychosis 20, 22-4, 70, 91, 104, 123, 161, 198

symptoms of 8, 24

psychosurgery 7-8, 29-30

psychotherapy 18, 21, 114, 159, 162, 182, 184, 189, 193

S

schizoid personality disorder 39

schizophrenia 15, 23, 32-7, 42-5, 48, 54, 61, 64-5, 67, 70-1, 73, 76, 82, 85, 87, 95, 97-8, 108, 118, 120, 122-3, 141-3, 145,

153, 158, 160-1, 166-7, 172,
175, 182-4, 195, 198, 207
schizotypal personality disorder
39
selective serotonin reuptake
inhibitor (SSRI) 21, 29, 40
self-medication 23, 80, 107, 109-11
separation anxiety 17
social anxiety disorder 17

somatogenic theory 2, 5
stigma
public stigma 51-5, 123, 155, 157,
161, 167-8
self-stigma 57-60, 86, 88, 144,
148, 152, 157, 161, 163, 172-3
stigmatisation 41, 43, 45-6, 72,
74, 80, 84, 131, 155, 172, 188,
194, 207

www.ingramcontent.com/pod-product-compliance
Lightning Source LLC
Chambersburg PA
CBHW030429290526
45786CB00001B/201